THE BOOKWORM'S BIG APPLE

THE BOOKWORM'S BIG APPLE

A Guide
to Manhattan's
Booksellers

Susan Paula Barile

Columbia University Press
New York

Columbia University Press

New York   Chichester, West Sussex

Copyright © 1994 Columbia University Press
All rights reserved

Library of Congress Cataloging-in-Publication Data
Barile, Susan Paula.
   The bookworm's Big Apple: a guide to Manhattan's booksellers / Susan
Paula Barile.
     p. cm.
   Includes indexes.
   ISBN 0-231-08494-3.—ISBN 0-231-08495-1 (pbk.)
   1. Bookstores—New York (N.Y.)—Directories. I. Title.
Z478.6.N5B37   1994
381'.45002'0257471—dc20   94-8968
                                       CIP

Casebound editions of Columbia University Press books
are printed on permanent and durable acid-free paper.

Printed in the United States of America

c 10 9 8 7 6 5 4 3 2 1
p 10 9 8 7 6 5 4 3 2 1

This book is dedicated to my son, Mark,
and to Kathleen Mays,
who holds a gentle mirror.

Contents

Acknowledgments

The following have helped, inspired, and befriended me along the way: Michael and Lillian and David, Bianca Bakalar, the Bedford Street Athletic Association, Lisa Bernhard, Ursula Bollini, Jim Demes, Nat Herold, Gini Kopecky, Julius Lester, Lynn McClory, Barbara Romaine, Joe Rubino (and his Harley), Mary Shadoff, Cliff Simms, Michael Turits, Eve Zanni, many kind Manhattan booksellers, and especially Phil Bruno.

Thanks to Andreas Brown who opened up Gotham's door for a year, to my editor, Kate Wittenberg, for this unswervingly punctual chance, and to my parents for inspiring a love of books.

Inexpressible gratitude to my red friend, John Stadler.

This book is for New Yorkers and visitors who love to read, browse, and converse. It's for publishers to use so that they can better distribute their publications. It's for anyone living outside of the city who has been looking for a particular book and will now have an additional resource to contact. It's for booksellers who need to find a referral, or a book for a customer, or who just want to check out the competition. Most important, though, this book is for the book lover, regardless of what his or her relationship to books may be.

Manhattan is the publishing capital of the world. The city is home to well over three hundred booksellers, and many of them, because they're neither centrally located nor endowed with advertising money, go virtually unnoticed.

Writers have struggled endlessly—against poverty, against persecution, and especially against indifference. Publishers, however, are not their only champions—booksellers are as well. *The Bookworm's Big Apple* celebrates all booksellers, not

just industry legends like Frances Steloff. If this books helps to
open doors that the reader did not know existed, it will have
been successful.

The conversant clerks and dusty piles or cramped aisles
you'd find in city and country shops are being replaced by
suburban spreads—new bookshop doors now open into stores
that are bigger, brighter, neater, and computer-dependent.
Our choices are becoming standardized—standards that rarely
extend beyond mid-range commercialism, regardless of quantity on display. The bookseller's art of handselling, which keeps
backlist on the shelves and smaller presses alive, is disap-
pearing. Indifference will not do.

But now, to paraphrase Congreve, these words are getting
serious, and perhaps dull, and *dull* is not a word to describe
Manhattan's wonderful abundance of booksellers. Here's to
those handselling personalities, and to your discovery and en-
joyment of them.

The Bookworm's Orientation

This book is divided into four sections: general, used, antiquarian, and specialty booksellers. For each seller who keeps retail hours I've included location (cross-street or avenue is in parentheses—avenues are always spelled out—with neighborhood name), phone number, fax when available, and store hours. A brief description is offered, and then a listing of the stock by section (words used to describe main and other highlighted sections are the store's, not mine). Many shops provide a shipping service, which usually means the store accepts both phone and mail orders. It may also mean that if you visit the shop and purchase a number of books, they'll send them home for you. If a shop does not have the book you want, many will special order it for you, either from the publisher, from a distributor, or even from another store. Sometimes there is a charge for this service.

The stock inside general bookstores consists primarily of new and unused books. (Note that many of them carry sidelines that are not discussed here and most will gift wrap your purchase.) Used books are those that have been read or previously sold. When a certain title is rare, or out-of-print, or very old, it is sold by antiquarian dealers. Of course there's always a snag, and in bookselling it's the modern *first edition*. The title may or may not be in print and may or may not be used, but it is always the book's first printing. The value of these depends on scarcity and overall condition of the book and dust jacket. You'll find sellers of modern firsts in every section of this guide.If a bookseller specializes in a subject—regardless of whether they sell new, used, or antiquarian volumes, or any combination of them—they are listed under specialty. You'll find that most of these dealers will search for the book you want if they do not stock it. At the end of each division a cross-reference is made to general or used shops only when their stock of the particular subject is extensive.

As for the words used here to describe books: *mass-market* refers to those little paperbacks you see in supermarkets and drug stores on revolving racks, *trade paperbacks* are larger in size, and the word *trade* in general is used to distinguish them from *university press books* or *textbooks*. Speaking of university press books, they are produced by the many publishing houses on campuses across the country. Most of the titles are by professors or professionals, yet many university presses publish fiction or poetry; often they will publish regional books. You'll find them in paperback and hardcover (paperbacks are soft and bendable, hardcovers—or *cloth editions*—are not. Usually the latter have jackets.) *Textbooks* refers to those oversize and expensive books used in classrooms. When a publisher produces too many of one title or decides to sell off a quantity of one book, this is called *remaindering*—hence, *remainders*.

Small press books are those provided by small publishing houses—they are usually nonprofit, although many are not—and the overall quality of the book, both in form and content, is typically good. When a publisher decides not to print a title anymore, it is declared *out-of-print*.

And finally there is the *antiquarian* or *rare* book. It may be a volume published hundreds of years ago or it may be the first printing of an author's first book. It may be bound in leather or missing a dust jacket. It may be in parts (like a serialized Dickens novel) or it may fall within the category of incunabula—books printed before 1500. What it definitely is is collectible and valuable. At the back of this guide is a listing of book fairs. Attending one is a great way to become acquainted with the antiquarian book market if you are not so already.

Booksellers who are open "by appointment only" sometimes sell out of their homes or restricted office space. Many have other jobs or attend fairs around the country. Most of them will gladly facilitate your visit, but you must call first.

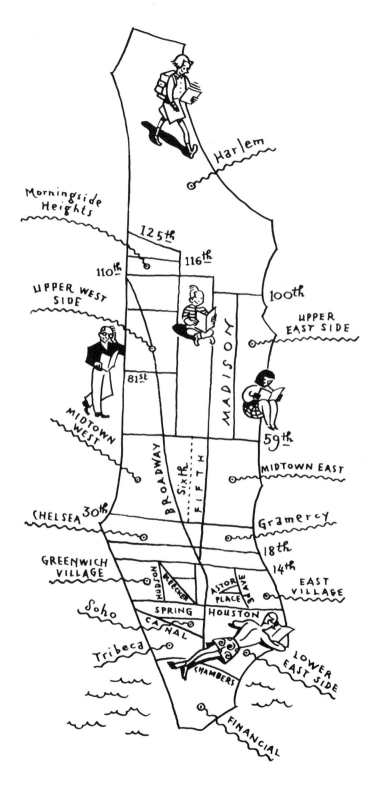

Harlem

Morningside Heights

125th

116th

110th

100th

UPPER WEST SIDE

UPPER EAST SIDE

MADISON

81st

MIDTOWN WEST

59th

BROADWAY

Sixth

Fifth

MIDTOWN EAST

CHELSEA 30th

Gramercy

18th

GREENWICH VILLAGE

14th

HUDSON

BLEECKER

ASTOR PLACE

EAST VILLAGE

Soho

SPRING

HOUSTON

CANAL

Tribeca

CHAMBERS

LOWER EAST SIDE

FINANCIAL

THE BOOKWORM'S BIG APPLE

G
E
N
E
R
A
L

Barnard Bookforum

2955 Broadway 10025 (116-Morningside Heights)
749-5535 (fax 932-3172)
M-F 9–11, Sat 10–8, Sun 11–7

Servicing the Columbia University community as well as the
neighborhood of Morningside Heights, the Bookforum has
one of the finest collections of scholarly books in the city, with
a strong emphasis on philosophy and criticism. Every section
is well-stocked with trade and university presses. At the time
of this writing the store is expanding its collection of small
presses and scholarly remainders, which are displayed on several sidewalk tables. Academic new releases are exhibited at the
front of the shop, Penguin and Norton Critical editions are
highlighted, and several university presses have their own sections. The basement is the home of hundreds of required course
books for Columbia and Barnard.

MAIN SECTIONS • Afro-American studies/American history/anthropol-
ogy/art/architecture/Asian studies/classics/drama/European history/film/

literary criticism/literature/Marxism/mathematics/Mideast studies/mystery/mythology/new releases—hardcover, paperback, university press/New York/philosophy/poetry/political science/psychology/reference/Russian Studies/science/sci-fi/Shakespeare/sociology/travel/women's studies

OTHER HIGHLIGHTED SECTIONS • cookbooks/educational outlines/ health/linguistics/media/music/nature/occult/parenting

SERVICES • author signings/shipping/special orders

Barnes and Noble

105 Fifth Ave 10003 (18th-Chelsea)
675-5500
M-F 9:30–7:45, Sat 9:30–6:45, Sun 11–5:45

While it doesn't have the record for most titles or longest shelving (that belongs to London's W and G Foyle with thirty miles), according to the 1993 edition of the *Guinness Book of Records*, Barnes and Noble is the largest, most spacious bookstore in the world, with 154,250 square feet. In fact, it is comprised of two sites on either side of Fifth Avenue. On the east side stands the main shop, and the "sales annex" faces it on the west.

B and N began as a textbook retailer in 1873, with branches eventually opening on college campuses throughout the U.S. In its textbook department, located in a room at the rear of the east side store, both new and used textbooks can be purchased (used at a 25 percent discount). Any paper or hardcover text-book for almost any university class can be found here.

The other specialized area on the ground floor is the law book room, stocked for both students and professionals. The rest of the ground floor houses B and N's extensive collection of new, general interest, and scholarly books. Technical books can be found on the mezzanine, medical books on the second floor.

At the entrance is a stairway leading down to the "buyback" area, where B and N will buy almost any book you have to sell in decent condition. The buyback price for textbooks is preset by a guide, while nontextbooks are purchased at B and N's discretion. Pass this stairway, go through the turnstiles, and you're on the busy, bustling, almost catacomblike main floor.

Ground Floor

MAIN SECTIONS • accounting/African literature/American Indian studies/anthropology/astrology/biography/business—accounting, banking, business law, careers, economics, handbooks, insurance, investments, management, marketing, real estate, retirement, stocks/child care/computers/cooking and wine/crime, real/dance/dictionaries/drama/ecology/economics/education—AIDS, ESL, general, special ed/educational outlines/exam preparation guides/fiction—general, Latin American and Caribbean, Near and Far East/film/finance/fitness—general, running, weight lifting, yoga/folktales/foreign language/games—chess, crosswords, instruction books, reference/gardening/gay studies/health—addiction, death and dying, general, holistic, personal growth/history—ancient, classical, medieval, American, world by area/humor/journalism/Judaica/labor/linguistic/literary anthologies/literary biography/literary criticism—deconstruction, general, New Criticism, postmodernism, structuralism/literature/magic/management/Marxism/mathematics/media/military/music—biography, history, instruction, songbooks/mythology/nature/new releases—hardcover, paperback/New York/occult/performing arts/pets/philosophy—Eastern, logic, Western/poetry/political science-U.S., world by area/psychology—Freud and Jung, general/reference—including Bibles, concordances, lexicons, publishing, quotations, writing/science/screenplays/Shakespeare/sociology/sports/travel/video guides/women's studies

The computer section offers the following divisions: advanced programming/computer applications/computers and society/desktop publishing/disk application/disk tutor/personal computers/programming languages/spreadsheeting/telecommunication/Windows/word processing

TEXTBOOK DEPARTMENT •

Aisle 1—business

Aisle 2—education, health, nutrition, psychology, accounting

Aisle 3—mathematics

Aisle 4—chemistry, physics, biology, earth science, agriculture

Aisle 5—English, foreign languages, communication

Aisle 6—history, sociology, anthropology

Aisle 7—art, music, classics, philosophy, religion

LAW DEPARTMENT • law textbooks—hornbooks and casebooks/legal theory/outlines—including BL, Emanuel, Gilbert, NutShell/practical law/reference/statutes

Mezzanine

antiques/architecture/art—anatomy, clip, color, criticism, drawing, history, illustration, reference, techniques, theory/automotive/calligraphy/crafts/decorating and decorative arts/design/Dover/engineering/etiquette/fashion/graphic arts/home building and repair—carpentry, masonry, plumbing, wiring/jewelry/photography/stamps and coins/wedding/woodworking

The in-depth section of engineering books includes the following highlighted categories:

aero, air conditioning, chemical, civil, electrical, electronics, environmental, engineering reviews, fire science, industrial, machine shop, marine, mechanical, robotics, and TV/audio/radio.

Second Floor

MEDICAL DEPARTMENT • Among the medical instruments, white jackets, and anatomical charts for sale, Manhattan's largest medical book center includes the following sections:

AIDS/alcoholism and drug abuse/anatomy and physiology/anesthesia and pulmonary/biochemistry/bodyworks/cardiology/child therapy/clinical manuals/clinics/cytology and genetics/dentistry/dermatology/diet and nutrition/eating disorders/EMT/endocrinology/exam reviews/family and couple therapy/gerontology/health and society/health care/hematology/histology/immunology/internal med/lab methods/medical history/medical reviews and series including National Medical and Lange/microbiology/neuroscience/new releases/ob-gyn/oncology/ophthalmology/orthopedics/pathology/pediatrics/pharmacology/physical med and rehabilitation/psychiatry/psychological testing/psychopharmacology/radiology/reference/sex, marriage, and family/sale books/sign language/speech pathology/stress/surgery/toxicology/urology and nephrology/veterinary/women's health

The nursing books are divided into these sections:

basic science/diagnostic/fundamental/general/intensive care/nurse care planning/pediatric/professional/psychiatric/specialties

The children's department at this B and N location is now housed in its own shop adjacent to the sales annex. The B and N "Jr." store is listed under children's stores in the specialty section.

SERVICES • book buybacks, shipping, signings, special orders

DISCOUNTS • 10 percent off new release hardcovers, 30 percent off *New York Times* hardcover bestsellers

Barnes and Noble Sales Annex
128 Fifth Ave
open fifteen minutes later than its sister shop

The sales annex of Barnes and Noble is a virtual emporium of book stores, consisting of two floors of new and used books, remainders and reviewer's copies sold at discount. The rear of the ground floor houses the used book section, unfortunately not as large as it once was, but presently undergoing an expansion and still worthy of browsing time. Popular and scholarly remainders tables are stocked with new titles regularly and are on both floors. Periodic visits to this store usually lead to finding an affordable treasure.

Ground Floor

MAIN SECTIONS • bestsellers/gift books/magazines/new releases/New York/remainders/reviewer's copies

PAPERBACKS (NEW) • anthologies/fiction/horror/mystery—suspense/ new releases—fiction and nonfiction/science fiction—fantasy

PAPERBACKS (USED) • art/biography/business and economics/ childcare/drama/education/drama/European history/foreign languages/Judaica/performing arts/philosophy/political science—law/reference/religion/self-help/social sciences/sports—recreation/travel

HARDCOVER (USED) • anthologies/biography/black studies/history—American, Asian, England, Latin American, Mideast and Africa, military, Native American, Russian/literary criticism/literature/medicine/nature and gardening/New York/pets/poetry/psychology/science/self-help/social sciences/space/sports and recreation/technology and computers/travel—adventure, foreign, U.S./women's studies

Second Floor

HARDCOVER • current fiction and nonfiction

HARDCOVER AND PAPER • new and remainders: cookbooks/games/ humor/travel

HARDCOVER REMAINDERS • animals and nature/art/arts and crafts/ biography/history/literature/photography/reference/religion/science/sports

B and N branches sell New York Times *bestsellers, general popular books, and remainders at the following locations in Manhattan:*

750 Third Ave 10017 (47-Midtown East)
697-2251
M-F 8–8, Sat 11–6, Sun 12–6

One Penn Plaza 10119 (33 & 7th, Midtown West)
695-1677
M-F 8–9, Sat 10–8, Sun 10–8

385 Fifth Ave 10016 (36-Midtown)
779-7677
M-F 8–7, Sat & Sun 10–6

38 Park Row 10038 (Beekman-Financial)
964-2865
M-F 8–6:30, Sat 10–5:30

109 E 42 St 10017 (Lexington-Midtown East)
818-0973
M-F 8–8, Sat 10–6, Sun 12–5

170 Broadway 10038 (Maiden Lane-Financial)
571-3340
M-F 8–6:30, Sat 10–6

879 Sixth Ave 10001 (33-Midtown West)
268-2505
MThF 9:45–8:30, TuW 9:45–6:45, Sat & Sun 10–6

2105 Broadway 10023 (73-Upper West Side)
873-0819
M-Sun 10–8

*600 Fifth Ave 10020 (48-Midtown East)
765-0592
M-F 8:30–6:45, Sat 9:30–6:15, Sun 12–6

*2300 Broadway 10024 (83-Upper West Side)
362-8835
Sun-Th 9–11, F, Sat 9–12

*1280 Lexington Ave 10028 (86-Upper East Side)
423-9900
M-Sat 9–11, Sun 10–9

*These are the "superstores," carrying a larger selection of popular new titles and remainders. Barnes and Noble's flagship superstore is located on Broadway at 81st Street, having a large ground floor and a huge second floor extending the length of one city block. On the mezzanine level is its very popular cafe. Stock for the superstores (as well as for the smaller branches) is purchased from centralized offices, and the sections offered are not so very different from B and N's first store location on Fifth Avenue and 18th Street. For the best that Barnes and Noble has to offer, check out this original shop—the only B and N to buy independently—where you still have a chance at picking up something unique.

Benjamin Bookstore

408 World Trade Ctr, Concourse Level 10048 (Financial)
432-1103
M-F 7–6:30, Sat 10–4:30

One of the two bookstores in this five-building complex housing New York's financial center, Benjamin's strengths reflect its surroundings—it is especially strong in business. It also caters to lunchtime and commuter reading, selling hundreds of mass-market fiction, horror, romance, and science fiction titles. Most sections are stocked with paperbacks, with the exception of popular new releases, which take up the entire front area.

MAIN SECTIONS • business/children/computer/current events/diet—health/fiction—literature/history/horror/investment/management/mystery/new releases/romance/science fiction/self-help/study aids/travel

OTHER HIGHLIGHTED SECTIONS • biography/black interest/bonds—security/careers/childcare/cooking/entertainment/humor/New Age/New York/options—futures/real estate/reference/religion—philosophy/sales—marketing/sports/true crime

SERVICES • special orders

Biblio's Café and Bookstore
317 Church St 10013 (Lispenard-Tribeca)
334-6990
M-Sun 8–10

coffee
iced coffee
cappucino
espresso
cold drinks
muffins
bagels
sandwiches

fiction
non-fiction
children's books
magazines
mystery
biographies
history
political science

317 Church Street in Tribeca
at Church & Lispenard

"Breakfast, lunch and Bukowski" is the motto of Biblio's, Manhattan's newest bookstore café dedicated to serving the growing community of artists, writers, and readers of Tribeca. Opened just recently, the owners of Biblio's plan to expand its menu, magazine, and predominantly paperback book sections as well as offer live music and dramatic performance pieces. Tribeca authors and poets are featured in weekly readings held during "happy hour," and their published works are showcased on separate shelves. The goal of Biblio's is to stay as literary, local, and grassroots as possible.

MAIN SECTIONS • children's/fiction/mystery/new releases—hardcover, paperback

OTHER HIGHLIGHTED SECTIONS • anthologies—literary, poetry/
art/biography/history/poetry/pol sci/sale books/travel lit

SERVICES • readings, special orders
Biblio's will take on consignment any self-published literary works.

Bookberries

983 Lexington Ave 10021
(71-Upper East Side)
794-9400 (800-542-9400)
MFSat 10–7, TWTh 10–10,
Sun 12–6

When owner Lauren Astor decided to open up a bookstore in
1990, she wanted to offer her customers something unusual, a
service that would combine her love of books with, if possible,
a unique commercial angle. The idea she devised is proving
successful. Bookberries is the home of the gift book basket,
expediting shipping around the world for such occasions as a
new baby, wedding, convalescence, graduation, or just about
any event a customer desires to mark. Baskets of all shapes and
sizes are displayed above every section, which are not stocked
in depth but do demonstrate the buyer's appealing and literate
interests. The children's section is quite extensive, however,
due in part to the owner's background as an elementary school
teacher.

MAIN SECTIONS • animals—gardening—nature/belles lettres/biogra-
phy/business/children's/cookbooks/fiction/gift books/health/history/literary
criticism/mystery/mythology/new releases/performing arts/poetry/refer-
ence/travel/young adults

OTHER HIGHLIGHTED SECTIONS • childcare/philosophy/preg-
nancy/psychology/sports/travel essays/women's studies

SERVICES • gift book baskets (starting at $45), shipping, special
orders

Books and Co.

939 Madison Ave 10021 (74-Upper East Side)
737-1450
M-F 10–7, Sat 10–6, Sun 12–6

A few steps away from the Whitney Museum is Books and Co., renowned for its "wall" of literary writers, dramatists, and poets. Their works and works about them—ranging from criticism, anthologies, and biographies to essays, memoirs, and autobiographies—can be found in this floor-to-ceiling store-length section stocked with paper,

cloth, out-of-print, small press, and even some used books. Many of these titles are autographed.

The remaining fields of interest covered by Books and Co. are stocked with select cloth and trade paperback titles. A large selection of quality art and photography books, including entire works of several masters in every medium, can be found in the art section, while paperbacks stock the extensive history and philosophy sections. Literary new releases are displayed throughout the shop, where company is welcome for hours.

MAIN SECTIONS • architecture/art/biography/cinema studies/classics/ cookbooks/Everyman's Library/gardening/history-U.S., world, modern culture/Library of America/literature/Loeb Classics/Modern Library/music/biography, general, scores, theory/philosophy/psychology/reference/ women's studies

OTHER HIGHLIGHTED SECTIONS • anthologies/children's/mystery/ New York/travel

SERVICES • free delivery anywhere in Manhattan/mail orders/quarterly newsletter/readings/shipping/special orders

Brentano's
597 Fifth Ave 10017 (48-Midtown East)
826-2450
M-F 8–7, Sat 9–6, Sun 11–6

The lovely physical space of Brentano's once housed the Scribner Bookstore located within the publishing building of the same name, home of Maxwell Perkins, Hemingway, and Fitzgerald. With cast-iron fixtures and over 50 foot ceilings, the shop is a dream in beaux-arts, restored in 1989 to its original architectural splendor, designed by Ernest Flagg in 1913. And although Brentano's is now part of a nationwide chain (its parent company is Waldenbooks), this particular store exceeds the chain's standards and provides a fine range of general, popular new books.

Ground Floor
MAIN SECTIONS • biography/children's/health and childcare/history/ humor/literary anthologies/literature and fiction/mystery/new releases—paperback, hardcover/New York/travel—essays, world and domestic

OTHER HIGHLIGHTED SECTIONS • black studies/education/large print/literary criticism and essays/military history/poetry/political science/ science fiction/social science/transportation/true crime

Mezzanine

MAIN SECTIONS • art—criticism, history, monographs/business—advertising and marketing, careers, general, investment, cinema/cooking/gardening/management/music/nature/photo essays/psychology/reference—dictionaries, general, study guides/science/sports

OTHER HIGHLIGHTED SECTIONS • antiques/crafts/design/drama/ economics/fashion/games/gay studies/home design and woodworking/Judaica/law/mythology/Native American studies/New Age/performing arts/biography/pets/philosophy/recovery/religion/women's studies

SERVICES • corporate discounts, event calendar, preferred readers club, readings, shipping, signings, special orders

DISCOUNTS • 25 percent *New York Times* bestsellers

Waldenbooks has the following branch locations in Manhattan, selling New York Times *bestsellers at 15 percent discount, general popular titles, and remainders:*

931–933 Lexington Ave 10021 (68-Upper East Side)
249-1327
M-F 9–7, Sat 9–5, Sun 12–5

270 Park Ave 10017 (48-Midtown East)
370-3758
M-F 8:30–6

57 Broadway 10006 (Rector-Financial)
269-1139
M-F 8–6

614 Columbus Ave 10024 (90-Upper West Side)
874-5090
M-Sat 10–9:30, Sun 12–7

SERVICES • preferred readers club, special orders

Burlington Bookshop

1082 Madison Ave 10028
(81-Upper East Side)
288-7420 (or BUtterfield 8-7420)
M-F 9:30–6, Sat 10–6, Sun 12–5

Burlington
Bookshop

1082 Madison Avenue
New York, NY 10028

BUtterfield 8-7420
BUtterfield 8-7465

Manhattan's smallest pearl of a general bookstore lives within the Burlington shell owned by Jane Trichter. She directs an extremely knowledgeable staff and *fills* her modest-sized shop and maze of shelves with publishers' best, particularly in art, fiction, history, and new releases, as well as in the remarkably wide range of other sections offered within the store. Space is a bit tight, although browsing is encouraged. If you do not find what you're looking for, Jane is outstanding in locating it for you. Never have so many appealing new books, and some out-of-prints, been packed inside so small a space—Burlington's the proof that bigger is not better!

MAIN SECTIONS · art—biography, general, history/biography/business—corporate, economics, foreign trade, legal, management, Wall Street/classics/cooking/decorative arts/drama/gardening/history—worldwide, medieval, Renaissance, Civil War, World War I and II, Vietnam/Judaica/literature/music/mystery/new releases—hardcover, paperback/New York/parenting/poetry/political science/psychology/science and nature/theater and film—biography, general/travel—essays, local, national and international/women's studies and literature

OTHER HIGHLIGHTED SECTIONS · humor/Library of America/mass-market fiction rack/out-of-prints/reference/Zen and Eastern philosophy

SERVICES · free delivery (from 96–65 Streets, Fifth to the river), mail order, o/p searches, shipping, special orders, and, as one customer said, "keeps customers ongoingly happy"

Chartwell Booksellers
55 E 52 St 10055 (Park-Midtown East)
308-0643
M-F 9:30–6:30, Sat only during tea dances

Chartwell Booksellers is housed in the Park Avenue Plaza office building owned by Richard Fisher, who is rumored to be a fan of Winston Churchill, which perhaps explains the shelves of Churchill-related books and the fact that Chartwell bears the same name as Churchill's country estate.

The Churchill connection aside, Chartwell's is a small general bookstore with most sections comprised of hardcovers. It has a sampling of rare books and numerous volumes on automobiles, acquired from a now defunct motorbooks store.

Nineteen ninety-three marked the store's tenth anniversary, celebrated in true Chartwellian fashion—with music and tea. Even without an occasion to celebrate, Chartwell regularly sponsors Saturday afternoon tea dances in the Plaza, to which the general public is always invited.

MAIN SECTIONS • architecture/business/children's/collectibles/cuisine/ fine arts/gardening/history/literature/motorbooks/music/new releases/pho- tography/reference/travel

SERVICES • readings, signings, special orders, tea dances

Classic Bookshops
133 World Trade Center (Financial)
221-2252
M-F 7:30–7, Sat 10–5, Sun 12–6

Opened in 1982, this is the remaining Classic Bookshop in Manhattan since parent company W. H. Smith of Toronto decided to close the doors of its main midtown location. Stocked primarily with popular titles, Classic provides good reads, travel books, and financially related guides and tomes for its clientele. Located at the opposite end of the concourse from its only bookselling competitor, Classic suffered severe damage from the World Trade Center bombing, but has recovered and has since expanded several of its sections.

MAIN SECTIONS • biography/black studies/business/children's/comput- ers/current affairs/dictionaries/fiction/health and fitness/history—Ameri- can, general, politics/horror/humor/literature/music and performing arts/ mystery/New Age and astrology/new releases/reference/religion/sci-fi and fantasy/sociology/sports/study guides/travel/war/young adult

OTHER HIGHLIGHTED SECTIONS • addiction and recovery/Ameri- can Indian/art/career development/childcare/financial/food and drink/ games and puzzles/gardening/movie novels/nature/New York/philosophy/ photography/psychology/real estate/romance/science/transportation/true crime

SERVICES • author signings, shipping, special orders

Coliseum Books

1771 Broadway 10019 (57-Midtown West)
757-8381
M 8–10, TWTh 8–11, F, Sat 8–11:30, Sun 12–8

Coliseum derives from the Latin word *colosseus*, meaning colossal or huge. Today, the word *coliseum* invokes a large stadium or arena for sports or other forms of public entertainment. The Greek term, *kolossos*, signifies the end or finishing stroke, giving us the word *colophon*, the publisher's trademark sometimes placed at the end of a book. If a large space filled with thousands of different colophons is your kind of entertainment, then Coliseum Books is your kind of store!

Books are stacked, piled, and crammed on every shelf, even on several old-fashioned metal supermarket racks holding thousands of mass-market paperbacks. Shelves surrounding these racks reach to the ceiling and hold trade, popular, and many scholarly titles. Hundreds of popular and some academic remainders can be found downstairs, and those sections listed below as "other highlighted" are considerably well stocked.

The noise level is high and the store is anything but serene. However, in the center stands an information desk where helpful clerks wait to direct you.

MAIN SECTIONS • architecture/art/astrology and New Age/child care/ children's/cookbooks/drama/fiction/film—extensive general, bios/gift books/health/history/humor/literary criticism/literature/music—extensive general, bios, scores/mystery/new releases—hardcover, paperback/New York/Penguin classics/photography/political science/psychology/religion/ science/sci-fi/sociology/theater arts/travel/TV and media

OTHER HIGHLIGHTED SECTIONS • anthropology/belles lettres/Bibles/crafts/Eastern philosophy/environment/fairy and folk tales/gardening/ graphic design/Library of America/literary anthologies/Modern Library/ mythology/nature/philosophy/poetry/travel essays/wines

ON THE MASS-MARKET RACKS • cooking/fiction/gender studies/ health/mystery/psychology/romance/sci-fi/self-help/true crime

Lower Level

MAIN SECTIONS • bargain and remainder books/business/educational outlines/fitness/foreign language/law and secretarial/reference/sports
    The computer section is categorized as follows:
amiga/business applications/communications/desktop pub/dictionaries/ DOS/games/general/graphics/IBM/laser jet/Macintosh/networking/Norton Utilities/programming languages/quick reference/Unix/Windows/ word processing

OTHER HIGHLIGHTED SECTIONS • auto repair/collectibles/games and chess/home building/pets/real estate

SERVICES • phone orders, shipping

Cooper Square Books
21 Astor Pl 10003 (Lafayette-East Village)
533-2595
M-Th 9–11, Fr & Sat 9–12, Sun 11–10

Cooper Square Books is one of the largest independent bookstores in Manhattan, situated in Astor Place, where the East Village meets the West. Although it is quite near New York University, Cooper Square sells more popular than scholarly new titles, with large areas of the spacious store devoted to children's books, mass-market reading, and remainder and sale book tables that spill out to the front. The remaining sections are stocked mostly with trade paperback titles, and a variety of book-related sidelines can be purchased here.

MAIN SECTIONS · anthropology/architecture/art/biography/black his-
tory/business/childcare/children's—young adult/computers/cooking/
drama/educational outlines/fiction—mass-market/film/gay studies/health/
history/horror/humor/literary criticism/literature/music/mystery/new releases—hardcover, paperback/occult—New Age/Penguin Classics/philoso-
phy/political science/psychology/reference/religion/remainders/romance/
science—math/self-help/sports/true crime/women's studies

OTHER HIGHLIGHTED SECTIONS · animals/arts and crafts/codepen-
dency/creative writing/Eastern philosophy/games/Judaica/language/law
and secretarial/mythology/Native Americans/nature/photography/sociol-
ogy/real crime/women's studies

SERVICES · shipping, signings, special orders

Corner Bookshop

1313 Madison Ave 10128
(93-Upper East Side)
831-3554
M-F 10–8, Sat 11–6, Sun 11:30–6

Once the home of a neighborhood pharmacy, the Corner Bookshop has adapted the carved wood fixtures into shelving, creating a warm and old-fashioned atmosphere, augmented by the tin ceilings and ancient cash register. In business since 1978, and dedicated to serving its Upper East Side community, almost a third of Corner's offerings consist of exceptional children and young adult titles in almost all fields. Trade cloth and paper titles fill the remaining sections. In the fall the store sponsors an annual dog party for the neighborhood canines, with treats provided for their guests as well.

MAIN SECTIONS • art—general, gift books, monographs/biography/ children's—fiction, nonfiction, picture books/history—bio, general, U.S. and world, young adults/literature/mystery/mythology—adult and juvenile/new releases—hardcover, paperback/photography/poetry/science— adult and juvenile/travel—international, national, New York/young adult—fiction, nonfiction

OTHER HIGHLIGHTED SECTIONS • cooking/gardening/health/hu-mor/nonfiction general/parenting/pregnancy and childcare/reference/sports

SERVICES • free delivery within a fifteen-block range, house accounts, newsletter, out-of-print searches, readings, shipping, special orders

B. Dalton's Bookseller

666 Fifth Ave 10103 (52-Midtown West)
247-1740
M-F 8:30–7, Sat 9–6:30

Now a division of Barnes and Noble, this is the flagship store of the nationwide chain of B. Dalton's. Only two remain in

New York—this huge store, which uses transparent promotional gimmicks like having an author write in the store window, and its recently remodeled Greenwich Village location. Dalton's sells a wide variety of cloth, trade, and mass-market paperbacks, with some university and small presses interspersed. Of note is the collection of books in foreign languages, and the medical and technical books offered.

MAIN SECTIONS · art—criticism, history, monographs, technique/biography/business—careers, economics, general, management, personal financing and investment, reference, small businesses/children's and young adult/college preparation and test guides/cooking—worldwide by region, diet and nutrition, wines/current affairs/dance/drama/electronics/engineering/fantasy/fiction and literature/film/gardening/health/history—American, Asian, Civil War, Latin America, Mideast, military, Native American, world/medical/music—general, blues, classical, jazz, rock and roll, songbooks/mystery/nature-general, field guides/new releases—hardcover, paperback/New York/parenting, childcare, pregnancy/philosophy—Eastern and Western/photography/psychology/reference—dictionaries, general, language skills, writing and publishing/religion/science/sci-fi/self-help/sports/theater arts/travel—worldwide by region, essays

OTHER HIGHLIGHTED SECTIONS · AIDS/animals/anthologies/anthropology/antiques/architecture/astrology/astronomy/bargain books/books in other languages/education/espionage—techno thrillers/etiquette/fashion/

fitness/gay and lesbian studies/hobbies and crafts/house and home/interior design/large print/literary criticism/mathematics/mythology/new age/Penguin Classics/poetry/real estate/sexuality/transportation/true crime/ women's studies

The computer section includes:

advanced, business applications, databases, desktop publishing, graphics, hardware, operation systems, programming systems, Windows, word processing

SERVICES • Book-Saver's Club (10 percent discount), shipping, signings, special orders

DISCOUNTS • 25 percent *New York Times* bestsellers

Discount Books

897 First Ave 10022 (50-Upper East Side)
751-3839
M-F 12–10, Sat 12–8

The Discount Bookstore is old-fashioned in every good sense of the word. The large and well-stocked store contains quality trade and scholarly texts; only a few popular titles are interspersed. Out-of-print titles and backlist hardcovers remain on the shelves here (most stores return these books quickly to publishers rather than keeping them for the customer's pleasure). The owner obviously has particular interests—the Mideast section and books on regional studies are excellent, as are the children's and literature sections. He also offers a choice selection of books in foreign languages. Even though the store is quite comfortable for browsing, you'll get the feeling it's not about aesthetics or displays or commerce; Discount is about books and customers—if the title you want is not here, the owner will get it for you, and if it is here, he'll discount it— 20 percent for hardcovers and 10 percent for paperbacks (15 percent and 5 percent, respectively, if you pay with a credit card).

MAIN SECTIONS • art—applied, biography, criticism, history/monographs, theory/biography/business and economics/children's and young adult—fiction and non/classics/college guides and test preps/cooking/ drama/health/history—Australia, Canada, England, France, Ireland, medieval, Roman/music—American, classical, Jazz, opera/mystery/new releases/parenting/politics/psychology/reference/regional studies—Africa, Eastern Europe, Central and Latin America, Soviet Union/sports/theater and film/travel guides and essays/war

OTHER HIGHLIGHTED SECTIONS · anthologies/Asian studies/black studies/card playing/computers/crafts/dance/decorative/design/etiquette/foreign language books/furniture/gardening/humor/mystery/occult/philosophy/poetry/religion/romance/sailing and aviation/science, nature, and animals/science fiction/sociology/westerns/women's studies/writing

There is also a selection of used mysteries and mass-market paperbacks.

SERVICES · shipping, special orders

Doubleday Book Shops

724 Fifth Ave 10019
(57-Midtown West)
397-0550
M-Sat 9–10, Sun 12–6

Only two stores of the original chain of Doubleday Book Shops still exist in New York; like Dalton's it has been subsumed by Barnes and Noble. This location is the largest. Not only is it an enormous space, with a glass enclosed elevator to transport you between floors, but the stock is equally extensive, providing cloth, trade paper, and mass-market books in the sections listed below. The travel, children, and young adult sections are exceptional.

MAIN SECTIONS · architecture/art—bio, ethnic, Far East, history, illustrated, museums, by period, reference, sculpture, technique/biography/childcare and pregnancy/children's and young adult/computers/cookbooks—baking, special diets, wines and spirits, worldwide by region/Everyman's Library/film/foreign language reference/gardening/gift books/graphic arts/health—diet and nutrition, general, transition and recovery/history—Afro-American, American, ancient, Civil War, military, Native

American, world/horror/humor/interior design and decoration/large print/
Library of America/Modern Library/music—bio, classical, general, popular, technique/mystery/nature/new releases—hardcover, paperback/New
York/photography/psychology/reference—dictionaries, general, writing/
romance/school and test guides/science/sci-fi/sports/theater/travel and trav-
elogues/women's studies

OTHER HIGHLIGHTED SECTIONS • animals/anthologies/antiques
and decorative arts/astrology/automobiles/aviation/boating and sailing/col-
lectibles/crafts/Dover books/drama/entertaining, etiquette, weddings/exer-
cise/fantasy/fashion/furniture and rugs/games/gay and lesbian studies/glass
and ceramics/inspirational/jewelry/Judaica/literary criticism/medicine/my-
thology/needlework/New Age/outdoors/Penguin classics/philosophy/po-
etry/religion/sexuality

Doubleday's new releases include
autographed titles/belles lettres/bestsellers/current affairs/fiction/mystery/
politics/short story collections/true crime

The business section is divided into:
accounting/advertising and marketing/biography/careers/economics/gen-
eral/international/investment/law/management/new releases/personal fi-
nance/real estate/secretarial/and small businesses

SERVICES • corporate accounts, shipping, special orders

Branch:
153 E 53 St 10022 (Lexington-Midtown East)
397-0550
M-F 8–7, Sat 11–6

Endicott Booksellers
450 Columbus Ave 10024
(81-Upper West Side)
787-6300
Sun, M 12–8, Tu-Sat 10–9

Encarnita Quinlan opened Endicott
Booksellers in 1982, just in the nick
of time for the Christmas rush. The Dominican laborers made
it home for the holidays, and Endicott opened to serve the
community with beautifully carved wood shelving, chairs, and
alcoves, destined to make it one of the most comfortable inde-
pendents in Manhattan. Now a co-op, the building used to

be the home of the posh Endicott Hotel, but had become one of New York's notorious SROs prior to the bookstore's opening.

The emphasis in Endicott is on literature and the humanities, with a notable amount of small presses and unique finds in fiction. Authors read here regularly, and Endicott suggests customers do the same.

MAIN SECTIONS • art—general, history, monographs/business/children's and young adult/collectibles/Everyman's/film/food and wine/health/history/Library of America/literary criticism/literature/Modern Library/music/mystery/new releases—hardcover, paperback/philosophy/photography/poetry/political and social issues/psychology/theater, dance, and drama/travel—worldwide by region, essays

OTHER HIGHLIGHTED SECTIONS • anthropology/archeology/belles lettres/biography/games/hobbies/home/mythology/nature/reference/religion/sale books/science/sports/TV

SERVICES • free delivery anywhere in Manhattan, newsletter, readings, shipping, signings, special orders

Gotham Book Mart

41 W 47 St 10036 (Fifth-Midtown West)
719-4448
M-F 9:30–6:30, Sat 9:30–6

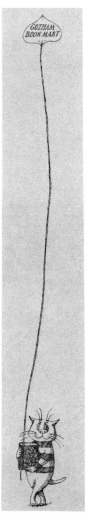

A New York literary institution, the Gotham
is not merely a bookstore. Founded by Frances
Steloff in 1920, the Gotham has been the
home of New York City literati and the center
of anticensorship since Ms. Steloff sold the
works of such writers as James Joyce and
Henry Miller, when they were otherwise un-
available in this country. Artist John Held's
sign "Wise Men Fish Here" hangs outside
this jewel, which is smack in the center of
New York's diamond district. The stock
mainly consists of literature, poetry, drama,
film and literary journals, with all sections
containing new, used, out-of-print, and small
press titles. Dusty books are piled everywhere, and books are shelved behind books.
If you are looking for a particular literary or
poetry title, just ask and observe. The clerk
will disappear into the infamous basement and
eventually come back up, almost inevitably
with your request.

A gallery upstairs houses mostly out-of-
print art books. Its special shows during the
year include a Christmas tree display of rare
antique ornaments, an exhibit of photographic
postcards (courtesy of Gotham's present
owner, and postcard collector, Andreas Brown), and a show of
the work of writer and illustrator Edward Gorey.

MAIN SECTIONS • authors' sections—Beats, Goldsmith, Gorey, Joyce,
Miller, and more/dance/drama/fiction/film and film-related—bios, criticism, quarterlies, screenplays/gemstones and jewelry/literary criticism/
literary journals/literature/music/plays, playwriting, playwrights/poetry/
theater

OTHER HIGHLIGHTED SECTIONS • art/classics/Eastern philosophy/ history/Judaica/new releases—hardcover, paperback/occult/philosophy/ psychology/reference/religion

SERVICES • appraisals, library purchases, o/p searches, shipping, special orders

See SPECIALTY—LITERATURE

Grand Central
89 E 42 St 10017
(Vanderbilt Ave-Midtown East)
687-5400
M-F 7:30–7:45, Sat 9:30–5:45,
Sun 9:30–5:45

Where do you think you are? Grand Central Station? Grand Central Books is a brand-new store, right inside the terminal, just across from the entrance to New York's famous Oyster Bar. The owners have provided travelers with an attractive, full-service store stocked mainly with paperbacks for commuter reading or long trips, hardcover new releases and gift books, and titles for the business person.

MAIN SECTIONS • biography/business/ children's and young adults/computer/cooking/crosswords/current affairs/exam guides/ fiction/film and TV/health/history—military, U.S., world/humor/literature/mystery/new releases—hardcover, paperback/psychology/ reference and dictionaries/romance/science/ sci-fi/sports/travel—domestic, foreign, New York

OTHER HIGHLIGHTED SECTIONS • architecture/art/astrology/careers/cars/chess/ childcare/codependency/collectibles/consumer guides/crafts/drama/Everyman's/fitness/gift books/health/gardening/law/Modern Library/music/

occult/pets/photography/poetry/pregnancy/religion and philosophy/true crime/westerns

SERVICES • corporate accounts, Send-A-Book, ship UPS, special orders

Madison Avenue Bookshop
833 Madison Ave 10021 (70-Upper East Side)
535-6130
M-Sat 10–6

Service is a key word for the Madison Avenue Bookshop. In fact it is so service-oriented—constantly receiving, shelving, packing, and delivering—that it almost resembles a small shipping and receiving room. However, don't be deceived—this emphasis on service and the hodgepodge extensive collection of books are exactly what has made the Madison Avenue Bookshop one of the East Side's most popular. Hardcover new releases and the extensive art section dominate the first floor, and a spiral staircase leads to the upper floor (which was closed for renovation at the time of this writing) where sections contain mostly trade paperbacks. Since Arthur Lobb opened this store in 1973 hundreds of personal accounts have been established, thousands of deliveries have been made, and, to this day, credit cards are not acceptable.

MAIN SECTIONS · art/biography/classics/cookbooks/Everyman's Library/fiction and literature/health/history/literary criticism/Modern Library/new releases—hardcover, some paperback/Penguin classics/philosophy/photography/poetry/political science/psychology/travel/women's studies

OTHER HIGHLIGHTED SECTIONS · business/essays and letters

SERVICES · delivery, mail order, personal accounts, shipping, special orders

Papyrus Booksellers

2915 Broadway 10025 (114-Morningside Heights)
222-3350
M-Sun 9:30–11

Ancient Egyptians, Greeks, and Romans made their first writing materials from papyrus, a tall water plant found in abundance along the Nile—hence, this store's slogan: "books started with Papyrus." For the present, Papyrus sells maps, literary journals, and a great deal of paperback books, both trade and mass-market, with some academic publishers mixed in. Hundreds of sale books and remainders are on outside tables, and if you continue around the corner, the basement (not accessible from inside the main shop) holds many more sections, including the computer books, medical texts, and all the study guides, Monarch and Cliff Notes the nearby Columbia University student might require.

MAIN SECTIONS · classics/cooking and diet/drama and film/literature/mass-market fiction/mystery/new releases—hardcover, paperback/Penguin classics/philosophy/poetry/psychology/reference and dictionaries/remainders/travel—national and international by region, New York

OTHER HIGHLIGHTED SECTIONS • Afro-American studies/Eastern religion/occult/romance/self-help and recovery/women's studies

Basement Annex

MAIN SECTIONS • architecture/art/business/childcare/children's and young adults/computers/history/math and science/music/political science/sci-fi/sociology and anthropology/study guides

OTHER HIGHLIGHTED SECTIONS • chess/economics/Judaica/Latin America/Marxism/medical texts/Mideast/Vietnam
   The computer section is divided into:
bestsellers, C programming language, D base, graphics, IBM pc, Mac, MSW, operating systems, Quatro Pro, Turbo/Pascal, Unix, Windows, WordPerfect

SERVICES • shipping, special orders

Posman Books

One University Pl 10003 (Washington Sq N-Greenwich Village)
533-BOOK
M-F 9–9, Sat 10–7, Sun 11–6

Collegiate Booksellers, Inc., has been serving college bookstores around the country for over twenty-five years, and under its president, Eugene Posman, this is its first independent, trade retail store, which recently opened in September of 1993, located in the heart of the New York University community. Posman plans to provide area students and faculty with a stock of scholarly presses in a range of academic fields, as well as neighborhood residents with more popular new releases, children's books, and general trade titles—all housed within a beautifully fixtured space.

MAIN SECTIONS • African American studies/anthologies—literature, poetry/art/children's/cultural studies/drama/Eastern philosophy and religion/education/film studies/gay and lesbian studies/history—U.S., world/literary criticism/literature/mythology and folklore/mystery and suspense/new releases—hardcover, paperback/philosophy/photography/poetry/political science/psychology/reference—careers, college admissions, general, resumes, test preps/religion/remainders/science/science fiction/self-help/sociology/women's studies

OTHER HIGHLIGHTED SECTIONS • acting/addiction and recovery/
African studies/anthropology/archeology/architecture/Asian studies/classi-
cal studies/dance/economics/gender studies/Latin America/linguistics/
literary biography/media studies/metropolitan studies/music/Native Ameri-
cans/Near Eastern studies/New York/Norton Critical editions/sexuality/
theater

SERVICES • author readings and signings, shipping, special orders

Rizzoli Bookstore

31 W 57 St 10019 (Sixth-Midtown West)
759-2424
M-Sat 9–8, Sun 10:30–7:30

When Rizzoli was forced to move from its Fifth Avenue site,
where it had been for over twenty years, the architectural firm

of Hardy, Holzman and Pfeiffer Associates (of Cooper Hewitt and Rainbow Room fame) was hired with one main goal in mind—to maintain its Fifth Avenue elegance. They triumphed. Cherrywood cabinetry, marble floors, restored Adamesque plasterwork ceilings, custom designed carpets, chandeliers, and strains of classical music all contribute to the continuing tradition of Rizzoli's opulence.

Known for its wide selection of foreign language books (particularly in Italian) and art, architecture, and design books imported from around the world, Rizzoli also carries an extensive selection of travel books. Hundreds of magazines and newspapers, also imported worldwide, are for sale, in addition to the recordings of those wonderful strains you'll hear for hours as you browse unhurriedly.

MAIN SECTIONS • architecture/art—history and monographs/biography/children's/collectibles/cookbooks/design/Everyman's Library/fashion/fiction/gardening/gift books/interiors/Modern Library/new releases—hardcover, paperback/New York/Penguin classics/performing arts/photography/poetry/reference/travel—worldwide by region, essays

OTHER HIGHLIGHTED SECTIONS • animals and nature/sports/transportation/wines

SERVICES • Rizzoli Bookstores Club, readings (in Soho store), shipping, signings, special orders

Branches

454 W Broadway 10012 (Houston-Soho)
674-1616
M-Th 11–11, Fri & Sat 11–12, Sun 12–8

200 Vesey St 10281 (West Side Highway-Financial)
385-1400
M-F 8:30–8, Sat & Sun 12–6

160 E 60 10022 (Third-Upper East Side)
705-2156
M-F 10–7, Th til 9, Sat 10–6:30, Sun 11–6:30

Shakespeare and Co.

2259 Broadway 10024 (81-Upper West Side)
580-7800
Sun-Th 8–11:30, Fr & Sat 10–12:30

Before the Upper West Side was a fashionable place to live, Shakespeare and Co., named after Sylvia Beach's shop in Paris, opened to fill the literary void left after Bloomsday Books closed its doors at the same location. Notwithstanding the Upper West Side, the store is dukedom large enough and sufficiently popular to have been featured in a Hollywood movie. Now, it is the West Sider's fashionable hang-out. Replete with trade paperbacks, and some mass-market and university presses, Shakespeare stocks noteworthy fiction, travel, and personal growth sections. To maintain its neighborhood customer base, Shakespeare provides children's storytime hours, regular author readings, and a bulletin board filled with notices about literary clubs and discussion groups.

MAIN SECTIONS · art—criticism, history, monographs/biography/business and economics/childcare/children's/computers/cookbooks—worldwide by region, beverages, diets, general/drama/essays and letters/exam and school guides/fiction/film/gay studies/gift books/health/horror/humor/Judaica/literary anthologies/literary criticism/music/mystery/nature/new releases—hardcover, paperback/New York/nonfiction—contains mainly history and cultural studies/personal growth/philosophy—Western/poetry/psychology/reference—dictionaries, general, foreign language, writing/religion/science/sci-fi/sports/travel—national and international by region, New York, general, literature/true crime/women's studies/young adult reading

OTHER HIGHLIGHTED SECTIONS · AIDS/ancient history/anthropology/architecture/astrology/careers/crafts/education/Everyman's Library/field guides/fitness/foreign language books/gardening/graphic novels/healing/holy books/home/law/Loeb Classics/Modern Library/mythology and folklore/pets/philosophy—Eastern/photography/recovery/sale books/Samuel French selection/sexuality/spirit and magick/staff suggestions/TV and other media

SERVICES • children's storytime on Sundays, corporate and school accounts, neighborhood delivery, monthly promotional discounts, readings, shipping, special orders

Branch
716 Broadway 10003 (Washington Pl-Greenwich Village)
529-1330
Sun-Th 10–11, Fr & Sat 10–12

Spring Street Books

169 Spring St 10012
(West Broadway-Soho)
219-3033
M-Th 10–11, Fr 10–12, Sat 10–1,
Sun 11–10

Spring Street Books is the single general new bookstore in Soho. Well-stocked with magazines and literary journals, it also sells a good selection of art books, especially the oversized, gift types. Most sections contain trade paperbacks and some small presses, with an occasional university press. Boxlike tables hold new releases and remainders, and way in the back of the store is a small bookshelf of out-of-prints.

MAIN SECTIONS • architecture/art/cookbooks/drama/film/graphics/ health/history/literary criticism/literary journals/literature/magazines/music/mystery/new releases—hardcover, paperback/New York/philosophy/ poetry/political science/psychology/remainders/sci-fi/travel/travel writing/ women's studies

OTHER HIGHLIGHTED SECTIONS • anthropology/biography/business/childcare/children-young adult/computers/crafts/Eastern religion/ fashion/folklore—mythology/games/humor/Judaica/nature/occult—New Age/sociology/sports

SERVICES • author signings/special orders

St. Mark's Bookshop
31 Third Ave 10003 (9th-East Village)
260-7853
M-Sun 11–11:30

In its new location around the corner from its original home on St. Mark's Place, St. Mark's Bookshop continues to sell its renowned selection of small press and alternative publications. In addition to its core stock of finer popular titles, the shop's sections on cultural and critical theory, literature, and poetry (particularly the Beats), as well as those on social and political issues, excel beyond most other general bookstores' mainstream offerings. Self-published works are showcased; literary journals and magazines are for sale; a bulletin board is provided for community use; and the well-read staff know their stock.

MAIN SECTIONS • Africa and African American studies/anthologies— literature, poetry/architecture/art—anthologies, criticism, monographs/ Beat literature/cinema/cultural and critical theory/drama/history—European, U.S./literature/Mid-east and Judaic studies/music/mystery/new releases—hardcover, paperback/philosophy/poetry/political science/psychology/science fiction/travel/women's studies

OTHER HIGHLIGHTED SECTIONS • anarchism/anthropology/Asia and Southeast Asia/childcare/children's/cooking/Eastern philosophy/educa-

tion/film—technical/gay studies/health/humor/Latin American studies/literary criticism/media/mythology/Native Americans/nature and ecology/new age/New York/photography/reference/remainders/science/sociology/sports/theology/urban, economics, and labor studies

SERVICES • shipping, special orders, will take books on consignment

Three Lives and Co.
154 West 10th St 10003 (Seventh West Village)
741-2069
M 12–7, T-Sat 11–8, Sun 1–7

Housed within a warm, inviting, denlike atmosphere, you will find an exceptional display of literary paperback and hardcover new releases at Three Lives and Co. The owners' and buyers' interests are evident—the literature and mystery selections are

extensive and always suggestively appealing, as are the smaller
offerings of cookbook, art, and gardening titles. Autographed
volumes are often available because of the regularly scheduled
author readings and signings. Three Lives and Co. provides
one of the loveliest and most intimate spaces in the city to hear
a favorite author read.

MAIN SECTIONS • art/gay and lesbian literature/literature/mysteries/
travel

OTHER HIGHLIGHTED SECTIONS • architecture/cookbooks/garden-
ing/philosophy/photography/reference/women's studies

SERVICES • author readings and signings, shipping, special orders. (An
additional service—you can arrange to have the shop select and send a book
to your mom once a month!)

Tower Books
383 Lafayette St 10003 (Fourth-East Village)
228-5100
M-Sun 11–11

Tower Books sits on the second floor above Tower Video, which
is just a block away from Tower Records; records being the
original artifact for sale by this California-based company.
Resembling a gleaming, neon warehouse, Tower Books has

an award-winning magazine section and good selections of literature, children's books, and smaller new release displays. The remaining sections are not as extensively stocked and carry more popular rather than esoteric titles. Major Tower enticements—it's open late 365 days a year and every book is discounted: 30 percent off *New York Times* bestsellers and 10 percent off every hardcover, paperback, and children's book.

MAIN SECTIONS • action and adventure literature/African American studies/architecture/art and art essays/art instruction/biography/business—banking, investment, real estate, sales and advertising, small businesses/childcare/children's/collectibles/college and test guides/cookbooks—baking, general, regional, special diets/diet and nutrition/drama/ecology and environmental/fiction/field guides/film—TV—video/foreign literature/games/gardening/gift books/history—U.S., world/home building and repairs/horror/humor/legal—general, reference, taxes, wills, and estates/literary anthologies/metaphysics/motorbooks/music—bio, classical, general, jazz, popular, songbooks, technical/mystery/mythology/New Age/new releases—hardcover, paperback/pets/philosophy—Western, Eastern/photography/poetry/pol sci/psychology/reference—English and foreign language dictionaries, general/religion/romance/science/sci-fi and fantasy/self-help/sex/sociology/sports—baseball, basketball, bicycling, bodybuilding, fitness, fishing, golf, hunting, and fishing, martial arts/theater and dance/travel—local, international, and national by region, essays/true crime/women's studies/writing

OTHER HIGHLIGHTED SECTIONS • AIDS/anthropology/Asian studies/beauty and fashion/boating/careers/Chilton manuals/crafts/crosswords/economics/education/engineering/erotica/etiquette/gay, lesbian, bisexual writings/health—general and by particular affliction/interior decoration/large print/literary criticism, critical theory/math/natural healing/nursing/pregnancy/remainders/war and weapons/westerns/women's health
   The computer section is divided into:
business software/desktop publishing/general/Macintosh/operating systems/personal/programming languages/Windows/Word and WordPerfect

SERVICES • readings, signings, special orders

Wendell's Books

22–23 Eighth Ave 10014 (12th-Greenwich Village)
675-0877
M-Th 10–10, F-Sat 10–11, Sun 11–8

Wendell's is a very small, literate, and hip bookshop tucked away in the West Village that carries an in-depth selection of small presses in literature and the arts and only the best in popular books. While it is an inclusive bookstore, it does specialize in subjects concerning modern culture, and many of the general titles focus on alternative aspects of traditional thought.

New hardcovers are sold at 10 percent discount, and a small selection of literary journals are available (for a complete selection of journals and magazines, go to Wendell's second store just one block north).

The literature section runs the length of one long wall and is filled with a wide selection of classics, avant-garde, and quality fiction. The laissez-faire sections covers philosophy, economics, and business. A bulletin board is available for community use.

MAIN SECTIONS • biography/culture/essays, literary criticism/film—bio, history, criticism/history/laissez-faire/literature/new releases/plays/poetry/scenes and monologues/screenplays/sex—gender—gay studies/theater—theory, history/travel

OTHER HIGHLIGHTED SECTIONS • art and artists/dance bio/dictionaries/film—technical/health, aids/improvisation, comedy/literary anthologies/musical theater/musicals/New York/poetry anthologies/psychology/religions/screen and playwriting/Shakespeare/surrealism

SERVICES • special orders

And finally, there are

Macy's
Herald Sq @ 34th St 8th fl 10001 (Midtown West)
695-4400 ext 2362
Sun 11–6, MThF 10–8:30, TWSat 10–7

The last department store to do so, Macy's still maintains a book department on its eighth floor, with replicas of the New York Public Library's lions to greet you. There are many display tables and face-outs, and various sections are routinely discounted up to 30 percent. Needless to say, the stock contains very popular titles, but the selection of lower-cost children's books had some surprising and choice finds.

And

Harris Books
81 Second Ave at 4th St (East Village)

Harris is a street vendor with a small second-floor shop, which is not opened regularly, but best hours to try are during the late evening. He mostly stocks new books, some used, in the humanities and sciences, and the titles are more avant-garde than popular.

Also see PROFESSIONAL—MCGRAW HILL, USED—STRAND and ADDITIONAL LISTINGS

U
S
E
D

Academy Book Store

10 W 18 St 10011 (Fifth-Chelsea)
242-4848 (fax 675-9595)
M-Sat 9:30–9, Sun 11–7

Classical, jazz, and operatic recordings on LPs and CDs are in the center of the Academy, surrounded by shelves of used and out-of-print books. The humanities and social sciences stand out in this collection, which includes a good number of academic presses and volumes purchased by Academy's owner from private libraries. In business for over fifteen years, the Academy is one of the original shops in Chelsea's expanding book trade.

MAIN SECTIONS • ancient history and classical literature/anthropology/ architecture/ art/cinema/decorative arts/design/fiction/foreign language books/history—American and world/medieval and Renaissance studies/music/philosophy/poetry/political science and economics/ psychology/science and math/sociology/women's studies

ARGOSY BOOK STORE
Old and Rare Books

Argosy Book Store and Gallery

116 E 59 St (Lexington-Midtown East)
753-4455 (fax 593-4784)
M-F 9–6 (upper floors close at 5:30), open Sat Oct-April

The Argosy is a six-floor haven for bibliophiles, with well over a quarter of a million used, out-of-print, and rare books sold in an old-fashioned bookselling setting yet readily accessible through the computerized inventory system. Before entering the shop you'll find hundreds of books out front for a dollar or two. On the ground floor inside are books, book plates, and autographs for sale, in addition to an outstanding selection of prints on every subject. An area marked "select reading" consists of titles recommended by Argosy's staff members. More autographs, early prints, engravings and an extensive collection of antique maps can be found on the second floor. The shop's renowned collection of Americana, history, biography and uncommon medical books are on the upper levels. Literature and books on the arts are in the large basement.

Argosy was established in 1924 and has remained a family business. You'll get the feeling once inside that you'll be able to find any book you've been searching for, and the hospitable staff will provide all the time and help needed to do so.

Basement

atlases/belles lettres/biography/bibliography/classics/drama and cinema/ fiction/music/photography/poetry/sci fi/works of O. Henry, Kipling, O'Neill, and Shaw are shelved separately

Ground Floor

antiques/art/architecture/ceramics/chess/Churchill and Durant/children's/ cooking/drama/encyclopedias/fashion/fine binding/fishing/furniture/guns/ illustrated books/marine/metals and jewels/philosophy/poetry/press books/ selected reading/sets

Second Floor

maps/paintings/prints

Third Floor

anthropology/archeology/children's/cookbooks/curiosa/games/history/ humor/Judaica/medicine/mystery/nature and animals/occult/psychology/ reference/religion/science and math/Shakespeare/sports/travel/world wars

Fourth Floor

books in French and German

Fifth Floor

first editions/American history—Civil and Revolutionary Wars, state histories, Native American and black studies, law and crime, politics, Vietnam

SERVICES • appraisals, library purchases, o/p searches, shipping

See ANTIQUARIAN

Book Friends Café

16 W 18 St 10011 (Fifth-Chelsea)
255-7407
M-F 11–9, Sat & Sun 12–7
(kitchen closes 1/2 hour earlier)

In a salonlike atmosphere, surrounded by tables showcasing Edwardian, Belle Epoque, and Victorian books, afternoon tea, lunch, and dinner are served at the Book Friends Café. Occasionally in the evenings books and ideas are discussed and read during one of the café's "Conversations" hosted by literary experts and writers. The stock is small, concentrating mainly on hardcover fiction and biography, but the aromas and ambience are inviting.

MAIN SECTIONS · art/biography/England—Edwardian history and literature/fiction/Paris

OTHER HIGHLIGHTED SECTIONS · antiques/architecture/etiquette/fashion/history/literary first editions/New York/sociology/travel

SERVICES · literary events, o/p searches, readings, shipping

Bookleaves

304 W 4 St 10014 (Bank-Greenwich Village)
924-5638
T-F 12–9, Sat & Sun 11–8

Bookleaves is a very tiny shop in the heart of the West Village selling a selected variety of used books. Each subject is allocated a shelf or two of cloth and paperback titles. A selection of modern first editions is available, and a few boxes scattered around the shop hold some book bargains.

MAIN SECTIONS · anthologies/applied arts and crafts/architecture/art— American, annuals, miscellaneous, monographs, technique/bibliography/ biography/cinema/dance/ecology/fiction/history/Judaica/letters and diaries/ linguistics/literature/miscellaneous nonfiction/philosophy/photography/ plays/psychology/science/sociology/theater/TV/U.S. politics

Bryn Mawr Book Shop

502 E 79 St 10021 (York-Upper East Side)
744-7682
W-Sat 10:30–4:30, Th 12–7, Sun 12–4:30

This is one of those dusty, haphazardly shelved used book stores filled with cheap, popular books and great inexpensive bargains. Ten shops like this one are located along the East Coast and run for the benefit of scholarships for Bryn Mawr college students. Most of the stock consists of hardcovers, but some sections are duplicated with paperback titles. Only donated books are accepted here and the staff members are volunteers.

MAIN SECTIONS · Americana/art/belles lettres and essays/biography/children's/cookbooks/education/history—Asia, Europe, Far East, Russia/history and politics—U.S./literary criticism/literature sets/medicine/music—classical, opera/novels/oversized classics and miscellaneous miniatures/poetry/reference/romance/science and nature/theater, plays, drama/travel

OTHER HIGHLIGHTED SECTIONS · anthropology/antiques and collectibles/architecture/business/decorative arts and design/foreign languages/humor/law/linguistics/military/mystery/religion/science fiction/short story anthologies/sociology/sports/TV and radio/women's studies

Chelsea Books and Records

111 W 17 St 10011 (Sixth-Chelsea)
645-4340
M-Sun 11–7

Stepping down into Chelsea Books and Records, you'll feel as if you're entering a store that's been around for years, when, in fact, it's quite new. The front of this cavernous store holds a good selection of used books—mainly in literature and the social sciences. Thousands of jazz, classical, and rock LPs belonging to a record dealer who rents the space fill up the back. The book end of the business is the owner's, a kindly gentleman who is both eager to help and content to let you browse.

MAIN SECTIONS • architecture—criticism, history, monographs/art—criticism, history, monographs/biography/drama/foreign language books/ Heritage Books/history—U.S., world/literary criticism/literature/music/ philosophy/poetry/psychology/reference/science/sci fi

OTHER HIGHLIGHTED SECTIONS • chess/classics/cooking/Marxism/theology/women's studies

SERVICES • shipping

Green Arc Bookstall

Union Sq W @ 16 St (17-Chelsea)
201-659-3704
open 7 days a week weather permitting (closed in winter)

Green Arc is an outdoor used bookstore, located in stalls on the western side of Union Square Park, home to the Greenmarket, where regional farmers, food producers, and green thumbs sell their wares regularly. The stalls carry paperbacks and hardcovers in a variety of general subjects in addition to art magazines, cassettes, and CDs. Hundreds of paperbacks are featured at a very low discount on tables, while primarily hardcovers are in the kiosks along the sides.

MAIN SECTIONS • art/history—world, U.S./literary biographies/literature/mystery/philosophy/religion

OTHER HIGHLIGHTED SECTIONS • children's/film/music/occult/ photography

SERVICES • will buy books in almost any subject carried, but appointment must be scheduled

Gryphon Bookshop

2246 Broadway (80-Upper
West Side)
362-0706
M-Sun 10–12

As the chariot driven by Dante's griffin renews the world,
the books in this Gryphon celebrate the earth's peoples. An
outstanding selection of anthropological and sociological books
on indigenous and native cultures around the world can be
found here, with many older and unusual titles mixed in.
Sections on literature and the arts are also well stocked. Its
second strength, an extensive collection of L. Frank Baum,
stems from the owner's well-known Ozmania. Gryphon's physical narrowness and height makes for awkward browsing, par-

ticularly the fiction section, as shelves reach to the ceiling with only the center staircase to access the top shelves. But below the staircase, amidst the piles of waiting-to-be-shelved books, sits its remarkable anthropology section, a good music section, and jazz and classical LPs (only a fraction of what Gryphon has to offer—check out is complete record store on 72d. Street).

And, once in a while, one of the known-to-be-gruff staff members does take a liking to a customer.

MAIN SECTIONS • anthropology and history—Africa, Arctic, Europe, Egypt, North America, Pacific, South America/art/children's/fiction/music—biography, general, history, jazz, opera, pop/mystery/Oz/poetry

OTHER HIGHLIGHTED SECTIONS • antiquities and collectibles/ books on books/chess/cookbooks/occult/literary biography/New York/photography/plays/psychology/reference/science fiction

SERVICES • library purchases, o/p searches, shipping

Ideal
· 1125 Amsterdam Ave 10025 (115-Morningside Heights)
662-1909 (fax 662-1640)
M-F 10–6

Located near Columbia University on the second floor above a post office, the Ideal Bookshop is a well-hidden academic find, specializing in used and out-of-print scholarly works in theology, history, the Holocaust, philosophy, and literature. In business since 1931, Ideal's present owner purchased the shop over eight years ago, and has since developed an exceptional library of Judaica, Holocaust, and Christianity texts. Many of the books in these fields are located in a downtown warehouse that Mr. Lutwak will open by appointment only. However, the selection at the retail shop in these and most all of the main sections is extensive and exceptional.

MAIN SECTIONS • anthropology/biblical studies/black studies/china/ classics/drama/Eastern European studies/Hebrew literature—modern/history—American, British, English, French, German/Holocaust/Japan/Jewish mysticism/Judaica/Latin America/literature/math/Middle Ages/Middle

East and Islamic studies/philosophy—Eastern and Western/poetry/political science/Reformation/Renaissance/Russia—history, literature/science/sociology/theology

OTHER HIGHLIGHTED SECTIONS · Africa/art/Harvard and Heinemann Classics/Italian history/literature—German and spanish/Jewish feminism/psychology/reference/Vietnam/women's studies

SERVICES · catalogs 4x/year, library purchases

Landau's Books and Binding

33 W 17 St (Fifth-Chelsea)
229-0004
M & F 10–8, TWTh 10–9,
Sat 10–7, Sun 11–5

Books and Binding is one of Chelsea's newest, and possibly largest, used and remainder book stores. The spacious ground level of the shop will eventually hold close to one hundred thousand volumes. At present it is amply filled with remainders, higher-priced art volumes, and modern firsts up at the front, and used books in numerous subjects on library shelves from the middle to the back. The owner takes many books on consignment, which accounts for a good percentage of the stock, while the rest comes from his former store, which was, until the time of its closing, Queen's largest and oldest bookstore.

MAIN SECTIONS · anthropology/art—African, eighteenth- and nineteenth-century American and European, general, history, technique/biography/books in foreign languages/business and economics/children's/cooking/drama and theater/fiction/history—American, Asia, Central and South America, Great Britain and Europe, Mideast, Russia, U.S./literary criticism/literature/medical/music—classical, general, jazz, opera, pop/mystery/nature and ecology—birds, fauna, flora, gardening, general, oceans and fish, pets/New Directions press/philosophy—Eastern, Western/photography/poetry/politics/psychology/reference/religion/sale/science—astronomy, general,physics/short stories/show business and film/sports/travel

OTHER HIGHLIGHTED SECTIONS · African American studies/ancient history/anthologies/antiques/architecture/aviation/biography—literary, political/books on books/child care and development/collectibles/computers/design—graphic, interior/education/electronics/games, hobbies and crafts/gay and lesbian studies/health/home repair/humor/law/letters/marriage and divorce/math/Native American studies/needlecraft/sailing and boating/ sculpture/self-help/sexuality/Shakespeare/true crime/women's studies

SERVICES • bookbinding, consignments, o/p searches, shipping

The Last Word
1181 Amsterdam Ave 10027 (118-Morningside Heights)
864-0013
M-F 9–8, Sat 10–8, Sun 11–6

This is a general, used book store that stocks hardcovers and paperbacks in all sections, provides a selection of modern first editions among the literature titles, and caters to the Columbia University community. In the center of the store are tables displaying discounted books, with bins below holding jazz and rock records. Complete sets of historical, literary, and reference works are prominently displayed up front at good prices. The Last Word is the newest addition to the Columbia area booksellers.

MAIN SECTIONS • art/Bibles and biblical reference/black studies—literature and nonfiction/children's/drama/Eastern philosophy/Greek and Roman classics/history—American, China, European, general, Latin American, Mideast, military, Russia, World War II/Judaica/literary criticism/literature/music—biography, general/mystery/philosophy/poetry/reference/religion/sets—literature, reference/sociology/women's studies

OTHER HIGHLIGHTED SECTIONS • anthropology and archeology/architecture/biography/dance/economics/film and theater/fine bindings and illustrated books/foreign languages/humor/Marxism/math and science/mythology/New York/occult/photography/science fiction/sociology/textiles

SERVICES • library purchases, shipping

Mercer Street Books

206 Mercer St 10012 (Bleecker-Greenwich Village)
505-8615
M-Th 10–10, F 10–12, Sat 11–12, Sun 11–10

Mercer Street Books carries a moderate selection of used books in a wide range of subjects. The center of the store contains bins of used classical and jazz records, with some rock. They have very few first editions and rare books, which are for sale behind the counter. The stock contains more paperbacks than hardcovers and caters to its neighborhood, dominated by New York University.

MAIN SECTIONS · art/biography and letters/business and economics/children's/classical studies/computers/cookbooks/education/fiction/film—criticism, guides, history, journals, reference, screenplays/foreign languages/gender studies/history—American and European, military/language and linguistics/literary criticism and theory/Marxism, radical politics and labor/mathematics/metaphysics, New Age and occult/music—composers, essays, ethnic, jazz, opera, reference, rock/mystery, suspense and horror/philosophy/photography/plays/poetry/political science/psychology/religion/sociology/theater/travel guides and literature

OTHER HIGHLIGHTED SECTIONS · anthologies—fiction and drama/anthropology/architecture/Asia/astronomy/black studies/children's/crafts, interior design, and fashion/crime and law/curious and valuable books/dance/design/Eastern European studies/Eastern religion/electronics/environmental studies/games and magic/gardening and nature/health/humor/journalism/Latin America/media/Mideast/mythology and folklore/Native Americans/New York/pets/reviewer's copies/science/science fiction/space/sports and exercise/transportation/urban studies

SERVICES · shipping (with limitations)

Louis Nathanson Books

219 E 85 St 10028 (Second-Upper East Side)
249-3235
M-F 11:30–7, Sat 10:30–5

The sign above the entrance will tell you that this store carries "junk." That might be so, but in addition to some junk exists a modest collection of used books, mainly in the humanities and social sciences, comprised of mostly hardcovers with some paperbacks. In addition to what Mr. Nathanson calls the "eclectic" stock, there are art prints and ephemeral items for sale.

MAIN SECTIONS • art/biography/cooking/crime/fiction/history/mystery/science fiction

SERVICES • shipping

Pageant Book and Print Shop
109 E 9 St 10003 (Fourth-East Village)
674-5296
M-Th 10–7, F 10–8, Sat 11–7:30

Just around the corner from the once-famous and long-gone Fourth Avenue Booksellers' Row, between 9th and 14th streets, is one of its relocated and last survivors—the Pageant Book and Print Shop. The bi-level shop is filled with used books ranging from unusual and rare to just plain old and used. The first floor is home to thousands of antique prints and engravings, plus a wonderful collection of vintage maps, and a roped-off area of first editions where you'll need permission to enter. Upstairs is heaven. The selection of used books, piled high and double-shelved (that is, there are rows of books behind the ones immediately in view), is exceptional, especially in the history and literature sections. You'll also find hundreds of books for less than a dollar in the stalls out front.

Ground Floor
MAIN SECTIONS • antiques and crafts/architecture/art/aviation/biology and animals/cooking/film and photography/gardening/language and writing/literature and criticism—American, English, European/music/nature/occult/plays/poetry/sports/science/theater
   The first floor also features a small selection of reviewer's copies at half price, and hundreds of old National Geographic magazines.

Second Floor
MAIN SECTIONS • anthropology/business and economics/education/foreign language books/Judaica/medicine/military, naval and sea/mysteries/philosophy/psychology/radical and labor/religion/science fiction/sociology

Pageant's used collection of fiction is housed in several aisles of shelves on this floor; they are also double-shelved.

The history section is divided as follows:

twenties and thirties/Africa/American/Civil War/colonial/England and Europe/general/Latin America/Middle and Far East/New England/New York/Russia/west/world/World War I/World War II to present

OTHER HIGHLIGHTED SECTIONS · black studies/children's/curiosa/humor/journalism/law and crime/political science/romance novels/transportation/women's studies

SERVICES · catalogs

Reborn Books

238 E 14 10003 (Second-East Village)
529-7370
M-Sun 11–11

Inexpensive, gritty, busy, and crowded might all be adjectives used to describe Fourteenth Street. If so, what's inside Reborn Books is but a microcosm of its surroundings. The bookstore is very much like the block it's on, selling thousands of low-priced items, mostly paperbacks, with a few good bargains— but you'll have to wade through the piles of dusty books along cramped aisles to find them.

MAIN SECTIONS · animals/art/black studies/business/children's/classics/cooking/do-it-yourself/drama/ecology and nature/health/history— America, world, Hollywood and movies/humor/Judaica/literary criticism/music/mystery/poetry/psychology/religion/romance/science/sci fi/sociology/sports/travel/true crime

OTHER HIGHLIGHTED SECTIONS · anthropology/crafts/design manuals/Eastern philosophy/foreign language books/nutrition/occult and unexplained/philosophy/reference/self-help/sexuality/war/women

SERVICES · shipping

Skyline Books

13 W 18 St 10011 (Fifth-Chelsea)
759-5463
M-Sat 9:30–8, Sun 11–7

Skyline Books contains two large rooms packed with used
books, shelves to the ceiling, nooks and crannies everywhere,
stashes and piles all around. Thousands of books, from inexpensive paperbacks to moderately priced hardcovers to more
expensive first editions, can be purchased here, in addition to
the selection of classical, jazz, and rock records. Like the book
trade in Chelsea, Skyline too always seems to be growing—
customers are consistently greeted by boxes of books about to
be integrated into the burgeoning, inviting, and ever serendipi-
tous stock.

MAIN SECTIONS • art—American, criticism, history, monographs, museum, technique/biography—literary, historical/black studies/books in foreign languages/children's/cinema—biography, criticism, general, history,
reference/cookbooks/drama/fiction/graphic arts and design/history—American, Asian, Caribbean, Central and South America, European, military,
Russian, war, world/illustrated/literary criticism and essays/medicine/mu-
sic—biography, criticism, general, history, instruction,jazz, opera, refer-
ence/mystery/nature and garden and animals/New York/occult/philosophy/
photography/poetry/politics/psychology/reference/religion/sale books/sci-
ence/sports and games/theater—biography, criticism, general, history,
plays/travel—essays, guides/vintage paperbacks/women's studies

OTHER HIGHLIGHTED SECTIONS • anarchism/anthologies/an-
tiques/books on books/China and Japan/collecting/crafts/economics/fash-
ion/glass/Greek and Roman—history, literature/health/humor/journalism/
labor/Marxism/Modern Library and Heritage editions/mythology and
folklore/Native Americans/sailing and boating/sixties/Shakespeare/sociol-
ogy/true crime/urban studies

SERVICES • appraisals, catalogs, library purchases, o/p searches

Soho Used Books

351 W Broadway 10012
(Grand-Soho)
226-3395
M-Th 11–11, F & Sat 11–12, Sun 11–10

Soho Used Books is well-stocked—paperbacks and hardcovers reach floor to ceiling, display tables of remainders and further discounted books are piled high. Many of the nonfiction sections—including history and the sciences—are filled with more popular than rare titles, with a focus on books published in the twentieth century.

MAIN SECTIONS · anthropology/architecture/art—general, history/biography/children's/computer/cooking/crafts and antiques/drama and theater/fiction/film/gay and lesbian/history—American, world/literary criticism/medical/music—popular/nature and science/philosophy/photography/poetry/psychology/reference and language/remainders/sports/travel and travel literature

OTHER HIGHLIGHTED SECTIONS · astrology and occult/astronomy/black studies/business/chess and games/Christianity/dance/fashion/gardening/health—popular/history—ancient, military/humor/Judaica/law/math/music—classical/mystery and horror/mythology and New Age/physics/political science and current events/sociology/writing

SERVICES · shipping

Strand Book Store

828 Broadway 10003 (12-East Village)
473-1452
M-Sat 9:30–9:30, Sun 11–9:30

The story goes that when author George Will asked Strand's owner, Fred Bass, what the exact measurement of books was in the store, Mr. Bass replied, Seven and three-quarter miles. Mr. Will believed "eight" sounded better, and suggested using the figure in the store's advertisement. Fred Bass agreed, and the Strand Book Store, Manhattan's largest used (and new) book emporium, now boasts: "Eight Miles of Books"!

Two levels filled with incredibly well-organized warehouse shelves contain over two million used books, remaindered books, and even brand-new books that come into the store from reviewers. In fact, the Strand's collection of new books located in the basement at half-price is larger than that of many stores selling only new books. The regular purchases of private libraries are the source of Strand's thousands of reasonably priced used books, in every possible field of interest and study, and the extensive stock of remainders is displayed on the numerous tables extending toward the back of the enormous street-level space.

Founded in 1927 in a smaller location on Fourth Avenue, Mr. Bass is the son of the Strand's original owner. His staff now numbers close to two hundred, but he still occupies the main desk near the information desk at the shop's center. From this vantage point two branches have grown, a rare book department can be found three flights above, and one of the

world's largest and busiest used bookstores is overseen at eye
level. The Strand is a booklover's must.

Ground Floor

MAIN SECTIONS · ancient history/antiques/architecture/art history,
monographs, museums, technique, twentieth century, worldwide by coun-
try/biological sciences/black studies/computer/cookbooks/crime/decorative
arts and collectibles/dictionaries/drama/encyclopedias/fiction/history/inte-
rior design/Judaica/Latin America/law/literature/math/medical/Mideast
studies/Modern Library/music and dance/natural history/occult/philoso-
phy/photography/physical sciences/poetry/reference/religion and Bibles/re-
mainders—in all fields/sea and ships/sale books—remainders, half-price
paperbacks and reviewer's copies/social sciences—anthropology, education,
political science, psychology, sociology/travel/war

OTHER HIGHLIGHTED SECTIONS · aquariums/art—illuminated,
natural history, primitive/astronomy/atlases/automobiles/cartoons/cats and
dogs/ceramics/chess/children's/China and Japan/crafts/fairy tales/fantasy
and sci fi/fashion/field guides/furniture/gardening/health and beauty/Heri-
tage Press/humor/jewelry and watches/journalism/large-print books/Latin
and Greek/library science/literary reference/mystery and suspense/prints
and drawings/stamps and coins/toys/women's studies

Basement

Americana/architecture and design/art—biography, drawing, and painting,
history, monographs, reference, special discounts/books in foreign
languages/children and young adult/Civil War/economics and business/
Native American/New York/reviewer's copies—new fiction and nonfiction/
scholarly/self-help/sports

SERVICES · appraisals, library purchases, o/p searches, shipping

Branches
kiosks at 59th St & Fifth Ave and 59th St & Second Ave

and

159 John St 10038 (Front-South St Seaport)
809-0875
M-Sat 10–9, Sun 10–8

Tompkins Square Books

111 E 7 St 10009 (Avenue A-East Village)
979-8958
M-Sun 12–11

Located just to the west of the rejuvenated Tompkins Square Park, Tompkins Square Books is a small and sparsely furnished store with half its space dedicated to selling books, the other half to classical and jazz records. Perfect for late-night browsing, prices are relatively low, and the foreign language books and fiction selection, separated into hardcover and paperback, usually yield good finds.

MAIN SECTIONS • architecture/art/biography/black studies/books in foreign languages/film/history/literary criticism/novels/philosophy/poetry/reference/sale books/science/theater

SERVICES • shipping

University Place Bookshop

821 Broadway 9th fl 10003 (12th-East Village)
254-5998
M-F 10–5, Sat 11–1

The University Place Bookshop sits in a multiroom apartment, nine floors above Broadway, filled with used and out-of-print books in several general subjects, but its reputation is due to its extremely impressive selection of books on Africa, the Caribbean, and the black experience worldwide. Another aspect of its notoriety is the incredible disarray and dust, but the stock is so unusual that these obstacles are worth overcoming. Every African country is represented here in depth, as is each island in the Caribbean. The history and politics sections for every country are well stocked with many scholarly texts. The store also carries a wide variety of hundreds of political pamphlets as well as old literary magazines and journals.

MAIN SECTIONS • Africa—biography, history, literature, poetry, politics by country/African American literature and poetry/bibliography/biography/blacks in America—biography, history, military, race, sociology/Caribbean—biography, history, literature, politics/history and politics—Ameri-

can, Asian, European, Russian/literature and poetry/Marxism and Lenin-
ism/music/political studies/race/reference/South Africa—biography, history, literature, politics

The bookstore also carries an in-depth selection of books in original African languages including, but not limited to, Congolese, Swahili, Shona,
French, and modern Arabic.

SERVICES · appraisals, o/p searches, shipping

Also see ANTIQUARIAN, GENERAL—GOTHAM BOOK MART, SPECIALTY—LIT-
ERATURE

A
N
T
I
Q
U
A
R
I
A
N

and Illustrated Books,
Fine Bindings

Appelfeld Gallery
1372 York Ave 10021 (73-Upper East Side)
988-7835
M-F 10–5:30, Sat 11–4

Appelfeld's is an old-fashioned book store, one in which the staff is amiable and knowledgeable, shelves are filled with old and rare volumes, and torn pages and spines are mended. The narrow shop is filled with shelves holding works by American and English writers, leatherbound volumes and sets, and many illustrated and limited editions. Children's books, history, literature, and travel comprise the bulk of their stock.

SERVICES • appraisals, binding, catalog, repairs, shipping

W. Graham Arader III

29 E 72 St 10021 (Madison-Upper East Side)
628-3668
M-F 10–6

An exclusive collection of rare illustrated and colorplated books on early Americana from the seventeenth through nineteenth centuries along with antique maps and prints are housed in this two-room shop. Although retail hours are kept, the owner prefers to make appointments; browsing is a bit restricted.

SERVICES · appraisals, catalog

J. N. Bartfield

30 W 57 St 3d fl (Fifth-Midtown West)
245-8890 (fax 541-4860)
M-F 10–5, Sat 10–3

The integration of the late Mr. Bartfield's interests in leatherbound books and western art has resulted in one of Manhattan's finest art gallerys and antiquarian book shops. Nineteenth- and twentieth-century American and European paintings and sculptures have been added to the appealing collection of western art on display. And, while leatherbound book sets and fine bindings are a specialty of Bartfield's, the antiquarian stock now covers a wide range of subjects such as history, sporting, Americana, natural history, philosophy, and literature, including many illustrated and rare titles.

SERVICES · appraisals

Bauman Rare Books

301 Park Ave 10022 (50-Midtown East)
245-8890
M-Sat 10–7

In an alcove just off the lobby of the plush Waldorf Astoria Hotel is Bauman's Rare Books, resembling a stately and classic old-fashioned library. In glass cases, and on beautiful oak tables, you'll discover a collection of the finest and rarest (and costliest) antiquarian books, which represent just a fraction of Bauman's offerings—their main store is in Philadelphia. They acquire titles in various fields, particularly literature, history, and the sciences. Some of their recent offerings included Dicken's *Pickwick Papers* in its original parts for $6,000; Mrs. Mercy Warren's *History of the American Revolution* for $3,800, published in 1805; and Johnson's *Dictionary* for $19,500, published in 1755. Whether you are a serious collector or an interested browser, if you cannot afford the cost, you can definitely afford the time.

SERVICES • catalog, shipping

Compulsive Collector

1082 Madison Ave 10028 (81-Upper East Side)
879-7443
W-Sat 2–6

The fine antiquarian and rare stock of the Compulsive Collector is located on the balcony of the Burlington Bookshop. Since only a limited portion of the owner's collection is on view here, call if you're looking for a particular title. The Collector's stock is particularly strong in Americana, history, literature, Judaica, and travel, but he compulsively acquires in other fields within the arts and sciences as well.

SERVICES • appraisals, o/p searches, shipping

James Cummins, Bookseller

699 Madison Ave 10021
(62-Upper East Side)
688-6441 (fax 688-6192)
M-Sat 10–6

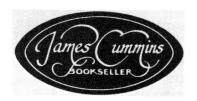

A distinguished antiquarian stock can be found at Mr. Cummins's shop with a concentration on literature, beautiful leatherbound sets of writings by historical figures, and illustrated volumes. The literature section has mainly nineteenth-century writings, with some moderns mixed in. Other categories on display include sports, Americana, travel, and exploration. The stock consists of truly rare and valuable titles, which explains Mr. Cummins's repute among book connoisseurs.

SERVICES · appraisals, catalogs

Imperial Fine Books
790 Madison Ave Rm 200 10021 (66-Upper East Side)
861-6620 (fax 249-0333)
M-F 10–5:30, Sat 10–5

The collected writings of political, historical and literary figures from the seventeenth to nineteenth centuries in fine bindings and leatherbound sets comprise the core of Imperial's stock. Owner Bibi Mohamed also specializes in rare single volumes in these subjects, with several autographed first editions mixed in. Antiquarian children's and illustrated volumes as well as art books from Asia are also displayed. Most of the books are so rare and/or beautifully bound as to make them rather costly.

SERVICES · appraisals, catalog, o/p searches, restoration, shipping

H. P. Kraus
16 E 46 St 10017 (Fifth-Midtown East)
687-4808 (fax 983-4780)
M-F 9:30–5

Early printed books, incunabula, ancient maps, and illuminated texts and manuscripts fill this five-story exclusive shop. This internationally known dealer in the rarest of manuscripts and books (the books available are only as recent as 1700) recommends making an appointment for the serious buyer, as only a small area of the shop is open to the general public.

SERVICES · appraisals, catalog, shipping

Weitz, Weitz and Coleman

1377 Lexington Ave 10028 (90-Upper East Side)
831-2213
M-Th 9–7, F 9–5, Sat 12–5

When the original Mr. Weitz won the Irish Sweepstakes he took his winnings and opened up a small bookshop where he sold and repaired rare volumes. Today, his son, Herb Weitz, and his partner, Elspeth Coleman, maintain a tradition of craftsmanship that is virtually unsurpassed. Classes in restoration are offered here, where binding, preservation, and design are done with the finest collection of tools. If you have a volume you wish to preserve, or are interested in purchasing a handsomely restored edition (Mr. Weitz's has a modest collection of antiquarian books for sale), consider this shop. Meeting Mr. Weitz is as impressive as Ms. Coleman's designs.

SERVICES • appraisals, library purchases, restoration and preservation, shipping

Ximenes Rare Books

19 E 69 St 10021 (Fifth-Upper East Side)
744-0226 (fax 472-8075)
M-F 9:30–5:30

The entranceway into Ximenes is somewhat drab and nondescript, which is why you'll be surprised when the shop door opens, and you enter a book-laden, librarylike room that owner Stephen Weissman has filled with rare and selective volumes. American and English literary works from the seventeenth to nineteenth centuries in addition to histories, travelogues, Americana, and science titles make up the fine collection.

SERVICES • appraisals, catalog, shipping

By appointment only:

Alexanderplatz Books
24 Minetta Lane 10012
877-1865

rare and out-of-print literature, modern art, photography, science, Judaica, and books within literary genres

Black Sun Books
157 E 57 St 10022
688-6622 (fax 751-6529)

focus of collection is on illustrated books, particularly twentieth-century French with original graphics, many autographed; also carries selection of rare eighteenth-, nineteenth-, and twentieth-century literature; catalog available

Bohemian Bookworm
215 W 95 St 10025
678-6011 (fax 678-6011)

"for book connoisseurs with small purses," books in a variety of subjects including adventure, cookbooks, European history, natural history, and travel (recently opened the Antiquarian Book Arcade in Chelsea at 110 W 25 St; call 620-5627 for hours)

Book Ranger
105 Charles St 10014
924-4957

has small general stock including Americana and travel; primary business is searching for out-of-prints in any field

William Boyer
Box 763, Planetarium Station 10024
724-9402

general used and antiquarian stock in variety of subjects including art and architecture, music, travel, history, theology, and
children's books

Martin Breslauer, Inc.
P.O. Box 607 10028
794-2995 (fax 794-4913)

medieval manuscripts, fifteenth- and sixteenth-century illustrated books, fine bindings; catalog available

James Carr
227 East 81 St 10028
535-8110

out-of-print and used in many subjects including art, books in
foreign languages, Christmas keepsake books, and works on
and about Mari Sandoz

Demes Books
229 W 105 St #46 10025
865-1273

uncommon and antiquarian books in many subjects, particularly literature, anthropology, and natural history and sciences;
will buy and appraise private libraries

Eastside Books and Paper
P.O. Box 1581 Gracie Station 10028
759-6299

general antiquarian stock of social sciences, some humanities,
particularly history (Civil War and Americana)

Donald Heald Rare Books
124 E 74 St 10021
744-3505 (fax 628-7847)

eighteenth- and nineteenth-century illustrated books on subjects including natural history, Americana, sporting, and voyages, art reference

David Malamud, Books
382 Central Park W 10025
866-8478

general stock including fine art, history, literature, music, New York City, and politics

Rostenberg and Stern, Rare Books
40 E 88 St 10128
831-6628 (fax 831-1961)

experts in the field of rare books and coauthors of books on the subject, R and S specialize in early printed books (1500–1800), history, literature, and political theory

Suzanne Zavrian
321 W 94 St 10025
749-5906

antiquarian, used, and uncommon books in many subjects, particularly literature and the arts; owner of the sadly departed Pomander Bookshop and founder of the New York Is Book Country fair

E. K. Schreiber
285 Central Park West 10024
873-3180 (fax 873-3190)

specializing in printed books of the renaissance, including incunabula, early Greek and Latin classics, and early illustrated volumes

Mark Solof
208 E 28 St 5H 10016
532-8749

used and rare books in variety of subjects within the humanities and social sciences

Alfred Zambelli
156 Fifth Ave 10010
734-2141

antiquarian and rare books on the Middle Ages, Renaissance, Reformation, philosophy, history, and paleography; catalog available

Also:

ARGOSY BOOK STORE (see p. 42 for complete description) has a highly regarded collection of rare medical books and Americana volumes in addition to a large selection of out-of-print titles in most of the subjects stocked in their shop.

LANDAU'S BOOKS AND BINDING (see p. 50) has a small selection of antiquarian and illustrated books in such miscellaneous subjects as history, literature, philosophy, poetry, and religion.

STRAND BOOK STORE (see p. 56) has a general selection of antiquarian and rare volumes in many fields of interest from the seventeenth century to the present. Enter the doorway to the left of the main store entrance, and three flights up you'll find their rare book room.

Architecture

Perimeter Bookshop
146 Sullivan Street 10012 (Houston-Soho)
529-2275
M-Sat 12–7

Perimeter Bookshop, one of Manhattan's two architectural bookshops, is located in historic Soho, a district that was once the center of New York City in the mid-1800s and now graces it with landmark cast-iron industrial buildings. Perimeter sells a complete selection of new books on architecture, with assorted titles on design and furniture, and sidelines of posters and postcards. The stock's focus is primarily on contemporary and modern architecture, categorized by subject, including books on architectural history, individual architects, and architectural theory. New releases are displayed on tables in the shop's center; imported and hard-to-find books are integrated on the shelves.

SERVICES • catalogs, shipping, special orders

Urban Center Books
457 Madison Ave 10022 (50-Midtown East)
935-3595 (fax 223-2887)
M-Th 11–7, F & Sat 10–6

Selling new books and periodicals in architecture, urban design, and historic preservation, Urban Center Books was established in 1980 by the New York Municipal Arts Society, in cooperation with the J. M. Kaplan Fund, as a service to the architectural professions and general public. It is located in the north wing of Villard Houses, six houses designed by McKim, Mead, and White in 1884 to look like a single Italian Renaissance palace, as commissioned by publisher, Henry Villard.

In addition to the topics listed below, Urban Center offers large sections of books on specific architects; architectural interest by period, e.g., Greek, Roman, Gothic, and Renaissance; by region, both national and international; by building type, private homes, religious structures, lobbies, etc.; and by century, eighteenth through twentieth.

MAIN SECTIONS · biography/construction/drawings/furniture and interiors/gardens/housing/industrial design/Modernists/new releases/New York/pattern and ornament/professional books/reference/theory and criticism/urban and land use planning

SERVICES · catalogs, shipping, special orders

And open by appointment only:

Arcade Books
Michael Sillerman
P.O. Box 5176, FDR Station 10150
724-5371

specializing in used and out-of-print architecture, design, and city planning books

For additional books on architecture, see listings under ART and DECORATIVE ART, and under MUSEUMS see GUGGENHEIM and METROPOLITAN MUSEUM OF ART

Art

Hacker Art Books
45 W 57 St 10019 (Fifth-Midtown West)
688-7600 (fax 754-2554)
M-Sat 9:30–6

How long has Hacker Art Books been around? If you ask its grand founder, Seymour Hacker, he would only be able to give you a glimpse into the past—the actual birth of the store is "lost in the midst of antiquity." Actually, it's well over fifty years old, and as cluttered and busy as ever. Thousands of new and unused out-of-print art books fill the shelves of Hacker's. Sections and shelves are not labeled. The store is arranged by subject, within each subject by artist, by cou ntry, by region, and/or by period, with first-rate history, criticism, and theory texts included. Books on technique, the decorative arts, textiles, pottery, furniture, jewelry, and graphic design can also be found on the shelves surrounding the tables of new release displays, magazines, journals, and exhibition information and catalogs. Hacker's is one of Manhattan's few full-service art book stores, whose benefits include the worldwide distribution of a catalog filled with art book treasures, some at excellent discounts. It is located one flight above street level on 57th Street near several midtown art galleries, and as a resource for anyone interested in the history of art its stock and staff can't be beat.

SERVICES • catalogs, shipping, special orders

Harmer Johnson Books
21 E 65 St, 4th fl 10021 (Madison-Upper East Side)
535-9118 (fax 861-9893)
M-F 10–5:30

Tribal and archeological art is the specialty of Harmer Johnson Books. Located in a townhouse, they sell primarily out-of-print books and objets d'art in an homelike atmosphere.

MAIN SECTIONS · African/American Indian/Ancient Near East/antiquities—Egyptian, Greek, Roman/Oceanic/pre-Columbian

SERVICES · catalogs, library purchases, o/p searches, shipping, special orders

Kolwyck-Jones Books on Art

588 Broadway, Suite 905 10012 (Houston-Soho)
966-8698 (fax 966-0413)
M-F 12–6, Sat 11–5

Kolwyck-Jones sells out-of-print artist monographs and art reference books, concentrating primarily on twentieth-century American and European art. In addition, they also offer a small selection of out-of-print books on architecture.

SERVICES · catalogs, o/p searches, shipping

OAN/Oceanie-Afrique Noire Art Books

15 W 39 St, 2nd fl 10018 (Fifth-Midtown West)
840-8844
M-F 11–5

OAN sells the largest collection of in and out-of-print books on pre-Columbian, Oceanic, and African art in Manhattan. On exhibit in their offices is a small display of commissioned tribal art, which is also for sale, plus hundreds of exhibition catalogs all related to this extensive collection of ethnological literature.

MAIN SECTIONS · Africa/Asia/Caribbean/general/new releases/North America/Oceania/pre-Columbian/reference/South and Central America/Southeast Asia

SERVICES · catalogs, o/p book search, shipping, special orders

Jaap Rietman

134 Spring St 10012 (Greene-Soho)
966-7044 (fax 925-5796)
M-F 9:30–6, Sat 10:30–6

Artists, not only writers, created Greenwich Village's bohemia; artists poured into the lofts of Soho and galleries flourished; artists of all mediums have turned Tribeca into Manhattan's new creative neighborhood. Jaap Rietman is the only full-service art bookstore catering to Manhattan's ever developing downtown imaginative communities, and has been doing so for over twenty years.

Throughout the store's loftlike space are large tables of new releases and some sale books. The shelves are filled with mostly new in print trade and small press books, and also hold an extensive collection of exhibition catalogs and art periodicals. Jaap Reitman is in the heart of Soho, one flight above street level, and is a wonderful place to spend browsing hours.

MAIN SECTIONS • ancient art/applied arts/architecture/art before 1900/ art deco and art nourveau/art of the twentieth century/contemporary art/design and graphic arts/new releases—hardcover, paperback/Asian art/photography/pre-Columbian and American Indian art/primitive art/textile art

SERVICES • catalogs, shipping, special orders

Ursus Books and Prints

981 Madison Ave 10021 (76-Upper
East Side)
772-8787 (fax 737-9306)
M-F 10–6, Sat 11–5

Ursus's logo, the bear, was the dominant image used in fine bookbindery by England's Earl of Leicester in the fifteenth and sixteenth centuries. And fine books—as conspicuous as Ursa Major—are dominant at Ursus, lo-

cated on the mezzanine of the stellar Carlyle Hotel, home to the famous Bemelmans Bar sporting murals by illustrator Ludwig Bemelmans.

Ursus occupies several rooms filled with library shelves holding new, used, and rare art books in both paper and hardcover, with one room devoted strictly to the sale of art prints. Catalogs are issued regularly, presenting both individual items for sale as well as collections of early printed and modern illustrated books. (Ursus is always interested in purchasing single art titles and collections of art reference books.) Their downtown location specializes in nineteenth- and twentieth-century art books and houses a second-to-none selection of exhibition catalogs.

MAIN SECTIONS · American art/ancient art/applied art/architecture/ book arts/by century—fifteenth to eighteenth, nineteenth, twentieth/collections/connoisseurship/ethnographic art/furniture/general topics/graphic arts/Islamic art/Judaic art/Latin American art/medieval art/metal arts/ monographs/Asian art/photography/porcelain and ceramics/prints and drawing/sculpture/technique and color/textiles and costume/theater arts

   In the rare book room:
antiquarian art books/architecture/early Bibles/gardening/modern illustrated/modern firsts

SERVICES · catalogs, library purchases, out-of-print searches, shipping, special orders

Branch
   375 West Broadway, 3rd fl 10012 (Broome-Soho)
   226-7858
   M-F 10–6, Sat 11–5

The following booksellers, specialties noted, gladly welcome visitors by appointment:

American Folk Art Books
   145 W 55 St 10019
   245-5042

out-of-print books on American folk art

Deja Vu
   30 Fifth Ave 8A 10011
   242-5154

books on poster and exhibition art, art nouveau

Ex Libris
160A E 70 St 10021
249-2618 (fax 249-1465)

antiquarian books on twentieth-century art, particularly 1920s
European avant-garde (graphics as well)

Leonard Fox
1790 Madison Ave, Suite 204 10021
879-7077 (fax 772-9692)

rare books on twentieth-century art and the fine arts

Eliot Gordon Books
150 E 69 St 8-H 10021
861-2892 (fax 838-0380)

art reference

J. N. Herlin, Inc.
40 Harrison St 25D 10013
732-1086

out-of-print books on art from 1950 to present

Barbara Leibowits Graphics, Ltd.
80 Central Park W 10023
769-0105 (fax 769-0058)

modern illustrated books

Mona Levine, Fine Antiques and Books
165 Park Row 12F 10038
732-9878

rare and out-of-print art history and monographs

Arthur Minters
96 Fulton St 2d fl 10038
587-4014 (fax 406-0867)

nineteenth- and early twentieth-century art and architecture

MJS Books and Graphics
9 E 82 St 10028
517-8565 (fax 650-9561)

Dutch, Russian, and German artists' books from early twentieth-century avant-garde

Oaklander Books
547 W 27 St, 5th fl 10001
594-4210

modern art, graphics, books on books

Elizabeth Phillips
108 E 38 St 10016
684-2369 (fax 684-6997)

illustrated books, modern art prints, photography, surrealism

Joel Rudikoff
300 Mercer St 10003
674-0219

antiquarian and rare art history and monographs

Two Sixty One Arts
261 Broadway 8A 10007
619-0869

new and out-of-print titles on twentieth-century modern art, with a focus on Latin American

Union Square Art Books
33 Union Sq W 10003
989-3083

general art

Andrew Washton
88 Lexington Ave 10G 10016
481-0471 (fax 861-0588)

out-of-print books on Renaissance and Medieval art

Michael Weintraub, Inc.
263 W 90 St 10024
769-1178 (fax 874-2481)

out-of-print illustrated books, architecture and decorative arts, applied art

Irving Zucker Art Books
303 Fifth Ave, rm 1503 10016
679-6332

modern French illustrated books

For additional art book sellers, see listings under ANTIQUARIAN, GENERAL—RIZZOLI, MUSEUMS—COOPER HEWITT, SOLOMON GUGGENHEIM, METROPOLITAN MUSEUM OF ART, PIERPONT MORGAN LIBRARY, MUSEUM OF AMERICAN FOLK ART, MUSEUM OF MODERN ART, STUDIO MUSEUM IN HARLEM, WHITNEY MUSEUM, and ADDITIONAL LISTINGS

Also, many art galleries throughout Manhattan sell books, particularly publications related to the artist on display. Some galleries of note are:

Galerie Saint Etienne
24 W 57 St 10019 (Fifth-Midtown West)
245-6734
T-Sat 11–5

This art gallery sells a limited selection of books and exhibition catalogs on German and Austrian expressionism.

William Schab Gallery, Inc.

24 W 57 St 10019 (Fifth-Midtown West)
974-0337
T-Sat 9:30–5:30

Housing an antiquarian stock of early art and architecture titles, the gallery also publishes a catalog twice a year entitled *Old and Modern Master Prints and Drawings.*

Howard Schickler, Fine Art

52 E 76 St 10021 (Madison-Upper East Side)
737-6647
W-Sat 11–6

Collection includes rare books on twentieth-century art, especially Russian avant-garde, and photography.

Artists' Books

Printed Matter Bookstore at DIA

77 Wooster St 10012 (Spring-Soho)
925-0325
T-F 10–6, Sat 11–7

Visiting Printed Matter, a nonprofit arts organization founded in 1976, is like visiting a museum. The store specializes in distributing books made by artists. Their collection currently numbers over fifty-five hundred titles, created by some twenty-five hundred artists. The artist is required to have been directly involved with the conceptualization, design, and production of each book, and then must pass the selection process for distribution through Printed Matter. Only a small number of small press titles are for sale. Printed Matter is one of the few places

in Manhattan where an original and unusual work may be purchased at an average price of ten dollars.

SERVICES • shipping

Other centers where fine and original books may be purchased are:

Center for Book Arts (Houston-East Village)
626 Broadway 5th fl 10012
460-9768

Granary Books (Prince-Soho)
568 Broadway Suite 403 10012
226-5462

Talas
213 W 35 St 10001 (Seventh-Midtown West)
736-7744

Asian

Asia Society Bookstore

725 Park Ave 10021 (70-Upper East Side)
288-6400
M-Th 10–6:30, F 10–8, Sat 11–6, Sun 12–5

With the goal of fostering communication between Asians and Americans, John D. Rockefeller III founded the Asia Society in 1956. The building, designed by architect Edward Larrabee Barnes, houses not only the bookstore, auditoriums for educational and cultural programs, and conference rooms where economic and political issues are discussed and debated, but is also the home of several galleries displaying an exquisite permanent collection of ancient and modern art as well as mounting exhibitions of public and private collections from all over Asia and the West. The bookstore carries a remarkable selection of literature translated into English from every region and country in Asia, as well as books written by Asian-Americans. The cookbook and art sections are also noteworthy, and if you're interested in origami, every book in print or kit on the art can be found here.

MAIN SECTIONS · art/children's/cooking/health and exercise/history and social sciences/language/literature—Central, Southern, and Western Asian, Asian-American, Australian, and Oceanianic, Chinese, Japanese, Korean/origami/performing arts/photography/reference/religion and philosophy/sale books/travel

SERVICES · shipping

And, by appointment only:

Asian Rare Books
175 W 93 Suite 16D 10025
316-5334

Out-of-print, old, and rare books on all aspects of Asia

If you'd like to receive a catalog listing antiquarian and used books of Asian-American interest, write to:

Yoshio Kishi
165 W 66 St 10023

For additional Asian booksellers, see FOREIGN LANGUAGES

Astrology

New York Astrology Center
545 Eighth Ave 10th fl 10018 (37-Midtown West)
947-3609
M-F 9–6

The small bookstore at the New York Astrology Center must be sitting in the twelfth house. Here you can purchase any book on astrology—books on the history of astrology, books on each of the twelve signs, books on how to decipher astrological symbols, books on how planets rule human activity, and books on famous seers through history. The moon's north node probably shines in here often.

SERVICES • shipping, special orders

For additional books on astrology, see NEW AGE, OCCULT

Audio Books

An increasing number of general and specialty shops offer books on tape. However, only one store exclusively sells

Audiobooks
125 Maiden Lane 10038 (Water-Financial)
248-7800 M-F 9–6, Sat 11–5, Sun 12–5

Heller Audiobooks stocks over three thousand books on tape, which are available for sale or rent. A wide range of fiction and nonfiction cassette titles include bestsellers, classics, mysteries, biographies, children's, business, self-improvement, history, and many more. Like video stores, they even offer a membership so you can rent at a discount.

Autographed Books

Each of the following dealers specialize in signed and inscribed volumes, concentrating mainly on literature, history, and the arts.
Call for an appointment or to receive a catalog.

Belanske's Autographs and Rare Books
245 E 40 St 10016
697-3091

James Lowe, Autographs
30 E 60 St Suite 907 10022
759-0775

Kenneth Rendall Gallery
989 Madison Ave 10021
717-1776

Tollett and Harman Autographs
175 W 76 St 10023
877-1566

Automobiles

No one store in the city specializes in books on cars, but the gallery L'Art Et L'Automobile, located at 121 Madison Avenue (645-6185) carries a fine selection of new titles on automobiles, in addition to graphics.

Also see CHARTWELL BOOKSELLERS (p. 14) and the section on TRAVEL.
Aviation—see MILITARY AND AVIATION

Baha'i

Baha'i Center and Library
53 E 11 St 10003 (Broadway-East Village)
674-8998

New paperbacks and hardcovers on the Baha'i faith are for sale in this center's small bookstore. Hours are limited and slightly irregular, so do call ahead.

Bibles

American Bible Society Bookstore
1865 Broadway 10023 (61-Upper West Side)
408-1200
M-F 9–5

The bookstore at the American Bible Society carries a complete line of Bibles in close to one hundred languages, plus biblical commentaries and American Bible Society religious publications. The society's gallery has a collection of rare bibles, and on display are reproduced fragments of the Dead Sea Scrolls and pages from the Gutenberg Bible.

SERVICES • catalog, shipping

New York Bible Society
172 Lexington Avenue
New York, NY 10016

OVER 180 YEARS OF URBAN EVANGELISM SINCE 1809

New York Bible Society

172 Lexington Ave 10016
(30-Midtown East)
213-5670 (fax 779-1076)
M-F 10–6

The Bible Society has been selling Bibles in New York since 1809. Presently they sell the New International Version and its corcordance in more than twenty-five languages. They also have available some King James and New American, but the NIV is their Main Book.

SERVICES · shipping (U.S. only)

See also CHRISTIANITY and JUDAICA listings

Biography

Biography Bookshop

400 Bleecker St 10014
(11-Greenwich Village)
807-8655
M-F 12–8, Sat 12–10, Sun 12–6

A well-lit corner shop directly across the street from a neighborhood park, the Biography is the only store in Manhattan specializing in new books on this subject. Biographies and autobiographies by figures in literature, history, and the arts abound, in addition to their essays, letters, and works. There is also a selective representation of new fiction titles, travel memoirs, and poetry.

SERVICES · special orders

And open by appointment only:

Biography House
547 W 27 St 10001
714-2004

specializes in out-of-print and rare biographies, diaries, autobiographies, memoirs, letters, and journals

Several different biographies of Theodore Roosevelt written for both children and adults, as well as books by our twenty-sixth president, are for sale at The Theodore Roosevelt Birthplace. Located at 28 E 20 St just off Park Ave, the house is open W-Sun 9–5. This National Historic Site is a faithful reconstruction of the original home, which was destroyed by a fire in 1916. Highly recommended piano concerts can be enjoyed on many Saturday afternoons. Call 260-1616 for more information.

Black Studies and African American

Black Books Plus
702 Amsterdam Ave 10025 (94-Upper West Side)
749-9632
TWF 11–6, Th 11–7, Sat 11–5

Black Books Plus sells a wide variety of new books in fields related to African American history and culture, and, with the recent inclusion of out-of-prints and used books, the stock is expanding. Sidelines include notecards, posters, children's games and toys, and folk art. Their selection of children's books written by African Americans is one of the best in the city, and the owner's experience as a librarian lends to her expertise as a resource in the literary fields. Author appearances are regularly scheduled (notables include Terry McMillan and Maya Angelou) and greatly attended, so be sure to arrive early.

MAIN SECTIONS • biography/children's/fiction/new releases—hardcover, paperback/nonfiction/women's studies

OTHER HIGHLIGHTED SECTIONS · cookbooks/drama/health/Malcolm X/military/religion

SERVICES · author readings and signings/shipping/special orders

Liberation Bookstore

421 Lenox Ave 10037 (131-Harlem)
281-4615
M-F 11–7, Sat 11:30–6:30

26th Anniversary
1967 - 1993
**LIBERATION
BOOK STORE**

"If you don't know, learn. If you know, teach." This is the motto of the Liberation Bookstore, in business for over twenty-six years in the center of Harlem. Liberation specializes in the history, culture, and politics of Africa and the African diaspora, and its selection on the arts is quite extensive. The shelves are stocked with paperback and hardcover titles, and some rare and out-of-prints can be found. Preferred writers run the gamut from mainstream (McMillan, Marshall, Mosley) to scholarly (Budge, Davidson, DuBois). In addition to the posters and calendars for sale, hundreds of pamphlets are distributed here.

MAIN SECTIONS · African history and culture/African languages/African American drama/African American family/African American history and culture/African American literature/African American music/African American religion/African American women/Asia/biographies/Caribbean studies/children's—fiction, nonfiction, activity books/cookbooks/dictionaries/education/health guides/know your enemy/labor/Marxism/military writing/origins of African American nationalism/poetry/political science/prison writing/racism/Reconstruction/slavery/sociology/South America

SERVICES · shipping, special orders.

At 260 West 125th Street there is a mini-mall of African American stores. Amen Ra and Isis sells black educational materials here, including a small selection of books on Africa, and African American history and biographies.

By appointment only:

Elvin Montgomery
519 W 121 St 3B 11207
666-4449

art, genealogy, history and politics, military, performing arts, social history, sports

Mosaic Books
Cathy Taylor
475-8623

African, African American, and literature from the Caribbean; catalog available

See also USED—UNIVERSITY PLACE BOOKSHOP, RELIGION—EMPIRE BAPTIST BOOKS

Bridge

Bridge World Magazine Books
39 W 94 St 10025 (Columbus-
Upper West Side)
866-5860
M-F 9:30–4:30

The publisher of Bridge World Magazine has a small shop filled with many new books on the game of bridge. The collection includes biographies of major players, game strategy, and history titles, alongside assorted bridge-related games and magazines. The game has been going strong here since 1929.

SERVICES • catalog, shipping, special orders.

Business

American Management Association Bookstore
135 W 50 St 7th fl 10020 (Sixth-Midtown West)
903-8286
M-Th 9–5:30, F 9–5

The bookstore at the American Management Association stocks a complete line of business and management books. Affiliated with Amacom Publishers, it carries all publications produced by this business press. AMA members receive a 10 percent discount on all purchases.

MAIN SECTIONS · accounting/business handbooks/career advancement/ computers/customer service/financing/human resources/marketing/personnel/self-improvement

For other stores where it's business as usual, see COLLEGE—BARUCH COLLEGE, IN-TERBORO INSTITUTE, PACE UNIVERSITY, TECHNICAL CAREER INSTITUTES, COMPUTERS—COMPUTER BOOKWORKS, PROFESSIONAL—MCGRAW-HILL, NYU PROFESSIONAL BOOKSTORE

Chess

Fred Wilson Books
80 E 11 St Suite 334 10003 (Broadway-East Village)
533-6381
M-Sat 12–7

Fred Wilson has been selling books on the game of chess—its history, masters, technique, and strategy—since 1973. New, used, out-of-print, and imported books on the subject are in stock, including those written in languages other than English. Periodicals and old chess magazines as well as chess sets are also for sale. Catalogs are issued regularly, and Wilson both appraises and purchases private collections. Your move.

SERVICES · appraisals, catalog, library purchases, shipping

Also:

The Chess Shop
230 Thompson St 10003 (Bleecker-Greenwich Village)
M-Sun 12–12

This is one of Manhattan's most popular places to sit and play a game of chess. A small café service is available, chess sets are for sale, and there's a good selection of books on chess both to purchase and to browse through.

Children's

Barnes and Noble Jr.
128 Fifth Ave (18-Chelsea)
633-3500
M-F 9–7:45, Sat 11–6:15, Sun 11–5:45

The children's departments at two Barnes and Noble Bookstores have expanded so greatly that they have become separate children's bookstores. B and N Jr. sells a great many popular children's books at a 10 percent discount, a number of audio tapes, toys, games and puzzles, and offers regular storytime hours.

Ground Floor
bargain books/black interest/Caldecott and Newberry award winners/Disney/Dr. Seuss/ethnic interest/fairy tales/growing up/learning center—teaching aids, workbooks, nonfiction/new releases—paperback and hardcover/poetry/pop-up books/preschool and board books/Sesame Street

Mezzanine
classics/middle readers/Tintin/young adult—fiction, series, thrillers

SERVICES • special orders, storytime hours

Branch:
120 E 86 St 10028 (Lexington-Upper East Side)
427-0686
M-Sat 9–9, Sun 11–7

Books of Wonder

132 Seventh Ave 10011 (18-Chelsea)
989-3270
M-Sat 11–7, Sun 12–6

Bats, goblins, princesses, and monsters fill the bewitching windows at Books of Wonder, and, once inside, a vast selection of new books, used books, out-of-prints, and rare illustrated books—many of them autographed—will prove equally captivating. Sunday afternoons are reserved for author appearances and storytelling. Oz is so beloved a land here that a club has been formed—The Royal Club of Oz—so that Oz-lovers everywhere can become members. If you're not a child when you enter Books of Wonder, you'll soon wish you were.

MAIN SECTIONS • board books/classics/Dr. Seuss/early readers/fables and fairy tales/first editions and rare—fiction and illustrated/foreign lan-

guages/minatures/myth and folklore/new releases—hardcover, paperback/
nonfiction—art, biographies, dictionaries, geography, history, sports/Oz—
hardcover, paperback, and rare/picture books by author/pop-up and flap
books/science/series—Asterix, Tintin/young adult—paperback and hardcover

SERVICES • author signings and readings, monthly newsletter, Oz club,
shipping, special orders

Storyland
1369 Third Ave 10021
(78-Upper East Side)
517-6951
M-Sat 10–6, Sun 11–6

Storyland is a sweet children's store with low-to-the-ground
overstuffed shelves filled with new books and wonderfully designed signs. Above the shelves and along the wall are original
and whimsical works of art presented to Storyland's owner
by illustrators and writers, such as Tomie DePaola and Uri
Shulevitz, who have made personal appearances at the shop.
Storytelling happens here regularly—on Wednesdays at 12:15
and Sundays at 1:30. And while the children are listening or
browsing, or eyeing the cassettes, videos, puzzles, and toys that
are also for sale, the expanding collection of first editions should
keep the adults properly entertained.

MAIN SECTIONS • baby books/classics/fiction-ages 1–10, 10 and up/his-
tory and biography/humor and activity/mystery/picture books/picture pa-
perbacks/science/sports/toddler books

OTHER HIGHLIGHTED SECTIONS • ABC and 123/arts and music/
beginning readers/cars and trucks/fairy tales/first editions/poetry and
Mother Goose/puzzles and games

SERVICES • author signings and readings, shipping, special orders, story
hours

The following children's rare and antiquarian book dealers are open by appointment only:

Susi Buchanan

325 E 79 St 2E 10021
288-4018

antiquarian children's and illustrated books

Jeryl Metz, Books

697 West End Ave 13A 10025
864-3055 (fax 222-8048)

used and antiquarian children's titles

Justin Schiller, Ltd.

135 E 57 St 12th fl 10150
832-8231 (fax 688-1139)

pre-1900 children's books in many languages

Myrna Shinbaum—Books

P.O. Box 1170 Madison Sq Station 10159
982-5749

antiquarian children's and illustrated books; J.M. Barrie

Many toy stores in Manhattan sell children's books; be sure to check the yellow pages listings.

See also EDUCATION—BANK STREET COLLEGE BOOKSTORE, TEACHERS COL-
LEGE BOOKSTORE, GENERAL—BOOKBERRIES, CORNER BOOKSHOP, DOUBLE-
DAY, USED—GRYPHON

Christianity

Adventist Book Center

12 W 40 St 10018 (Fifth-Midtown West)
944-2788 (fax 819-1973)
M-Th 9–6, F 9–1, Sun 10–3

The Greater New York Adventist Book Center sells books on all aspects of the Seventh-Day Adventist religion, with particularly well-stocked sections on children's titles and texts in Spanish. At the back of the store is a miniature supermarket of health foods.

MAIN SECTIONS • Bible lessons and manuals/Bibles/children's and young adults/Christian home library/death, grief, and recovery/devotional/doctrinal/health/home, marriage, and family/Spanish books/spirit of prophecy

SERVICES • catalog, shipping, special orders

Alba House Cornerstone Book and Gift Shop

16 Barclay St 10007 (Broadway-Financial)
732-4140
M-Th 10–5:30, F 8:30–5:30, Sat 12–5:30

This shop is located a few steps down and away from St. Peter's Church, the oldest Catholic parish in New York State, founded in 1785. Alba House (an acronym of the four gospels formed by incorporating the initials of the Latin symbols representing the biblical authors: Angelus, or angel, for Matthew; Leo, or lion, for Mark; Bos, or ox, for Luke; and, Aquila, or eagle, for John) also publishes a variety of religious books for children and adults. These publications, in addition to hundreds more new books of interest to the Catholic faith, are displayed.

MAIN SECTIONS • Alba House publications/Bibles/biography/Catholic authors/children's/church documents/liturgical/lives of the saints/Mary and rosary/prayer/religious education/scripture studies/self-help and healing/Spanish and other languages/theology and philosophy

OTHER HIGHLIGHTED SECTIONS · Eastern Orthodox/religious studies/women's studies

SERVICES · shipping

Calvary Bookstore

139 W 57 St 10019 (Sixth-Midtown West)
315-0230
M 3–9, W 12–7, Sun 12:30–4

It's not open often, but when it is you can find a selection of religious and inspirational books, with an emphasis on Bibles and children's titles. Other subjects covered include general religion, prayer, self-help, biblical commentaries, and general guides on the Protestant way of life.

Christian Publications Book and Supply Center

315 W 43 St 10036 (Eighth-Midtown West)
582-4311 (fax 262-1825)
M-F 9:30–5:45, Th -6:45, Sat 9:30–4:45

This is metro New York's largest Christian bookstore, in business since 1883, and stocked with gifts, cards, videos, cassettes, liturgical wear, church items, and thousands of new books. Bibles are for sale in a variety of languages, and the stock of books in Spanish is extensive.

MAIN SECTIONS · Bible studies/Bibles/biography/Christian life/ Christology/contemporary issues/cults and occults/devotional/discipleship/ doctrine/family and parenting/history/holy spirit/love and marriage/meditation books/New Testament/Old Testament/popular authors/preaching/ prophecy/psychology/sale books/science/theology/women

OTHER HIGHLIGHTED SECTIONS · apologetics/Bible studies/bibliology/business and economics/counseling/devotional fiction/reference/romance/study aids/teen books

BOOKS IN SPANISH · antiguo testamento/apologetica/ayudas/biblias en español/biografías/cristología/diccionarios and concordancias/ed. cristiana/

espiritu/evangelismo/familia/himnarios/manueles biblicos/novedades/
nuevo testamento/oracion/pastorales/santo/teología

SERVICES • shipping special orders

Empire Baptist Bookstore
121 W 125 St 10027 (Lenox-Harlem)
289-7628
M-Sat 10–6

The Bible is the focus of this bookstore. Empire Baptist sells
hundreds of them, including concordances, handbooks, and
texts on Bible studies. A smaller selection of works on black
history, in addition to hymnals, prayer, and children's books,
are also for sale.

Episcopal Book Center
815 Second Ave 10017 (43-Midtown East)
661-4863
M-F 10–5

Also known as the Seabury Bookshop, the Episcopal Book Center is a
large store with most of the new titles
devoted to nondenominational books
on religion. In fact, the sign out
front welcomes everyone, regardless
of race, color, or the number of
times one has been born.

T • H • E
EPISCOPAL
B • O • O • K
RESOURCE
CENTER

MAIN SECTIONS • Bible studies and concordances/Bibles/children's/
church history/ecology and greening of the church/ethics/human sexuality/
literary classics/mythology/religion/sale books/spirituality/theology/
women's studies

OTHER HIGHLIGHTED SECTIONS • church growth/homiletics/lit-
urgy/Morehouse publications/pastoral counseling/sacraments/youth education

SERVICES • shipping

Hephzibah House
51 W 75 St 10023 (Amsterdam-Upper West Side)
787-6150
M-Sat 9–5

This Christian guest house and community center, named in honor of the Bible's hospitable Hephzibah, has books for sale in the entrance parlor of this impeccably restored and maintained nineteenth-century townhouse. A small selection of prayer books, concordances, and books on spirituality and Christian living are available.

Living Word Books
62 Thomas St 10013 (Church-Financial)
571-7458
M-Th 10–6, F 10–7, Sat 10–4

On Sundays you can enjoy the "ultimate fellowship experience" at the open church services held at the Living Word Christian Center. During the week you can get the good news at their bookstore, which has a large selection of children's and young adult books, Bibles, and a wide range of new titles on Christian living and spirituality.

SERVICES · shipping

Logos Bookstore
342 Madison Ave 10173 (43-Midtown East)
697-4888
M-F 8–7, Sat 10–7

This is the only branch in Manhattan of the nationwide chain of Logos Bookstores, which provide a general range of new books but whose emphasis is on theology, spirituality, and the Christian way of life.

MAIN SECTIONS · Bibles/biography/business/children's and young adult/church history/classics/commentaries/cookbooks/fiction/gift books/ humor/new releases—hardcover, paperback/psychology/recovery and self-help/reference/science and nature/spirituality/theology/travel

Specialty • **99**

OTHER HIGHLIGHTED SECTIONS • African American studies/history/Judaica/missions and social issues/performing arts/philosophy/women's studies

New York Theological Seminary Bookstore
5 W 29 St 10001 (Fifth-Chelsea)
532-4012
M-Th 1–7, Sat 10–5

Half of the bookstore at this graduate school is devoted to texts for classes, while the second half offers a selection of new nondenominational religious titles. Bibles, meditational, and gift books are also available.

Paraclete   The PARACLETE BOOK CENTER
146 E 74 St 10021 (Lexington-
Upper East Side)
535-4050
T-F 10–6, Sat 10–5

Paraclete is quite a large store specializing in theology and Christianity. Sections are filled with mainly paperbacks, some hardcovers, and almost all of them are of a scholarly nature. The sections are quite broad in scope but are not labeled. However, well-informed and friendly staff members are there for assistance. The store, as its name from the Greek word suggests, is there for comfort.

MAIN SECTIONS • biography/comparative religions/education/history—general, medieval/liturgy/Lewis/Merton/ministry/saints/scripture/spirituality/theology/third world and social issues/women's studies

OTHER HIGHLIGHTED SECTIONS • children's/family/ecology/medical ethics

SERVICES • catalog, shipping, special orders

Paulist Book and Gift Shop
415 W 59 St 10019 (Columbus-
Midtown West)
315-0918
M-F 10–6, Sat 12:30–6:30,
Sun 10–2:30, 4:30–6:30

The Paulist Book and Gift Shop is actually located in the
Church of St. Paul the Apostle on Columbus Avenue. Before
entering the shop on the right the church itself is worth a visit.
It was architecturally inspired by the early Christian basilicas
in Ravenna from the fourth and fifth centuries, and some of
the artists who beautified its interior include LaFarge, Saint-
Gaudens, and Stanford White. The small and heavily stocked
bookstore concentrates on Bibles, the saints, Christian writers,
and the history of the Church.

MAIN SECTIONS · Bibles/catechisms/Christian authors/church history/
inspiration/personal growth/recovery/religious education/saints—lives,
writings/scripture/spirituality/St. Francis

OTHER HIGHLIGHTED SECTIONS · classics of Western spirituality/
ethics and morality/liturgy/meditation/other religions/philosophy and theol-
ogy/psychology/religious classics/women and the church

St. Francis Bookshop
135 W 31 St 10001 (Sixth-Midtown)
736-8500
M-Sat 10–6

The church of St. Francis, known as 31 Street's House of
Peace, is over 150 years old and is also home to a small
bookshop carrying new titles, mostly paperbacks, in a variety
of topics on Catholocism.

MAIN SECTIONS · Bibles/biblical studies/biography/devotional/family
issues/Franciscan/health and recovery/homiletics/inspirational/liturgical/
ministry/new releases/prayer books/psychology/sale books/sexuality/social
justice/Spanish/spirituality/women's studies

St. Paul Book and Media Center

150 E 52 St 10022 (Third-Midtown East)
754-1110
M 11:30–5:15, T-F 9:30–5:15, Sat 10–5

St. Paul Book and Media Center is a large Catholic bookstore carrying a wide range of subjects related to the church, the saints, and the Catholic way of life. The store sells many kindred sidelines, including but not limited to rosary beads, statues, and other religious articles and pamphlets.

MAIN SECTIONS • Bibles/biography/children's/church doctrinal teachings/marriage and family life/noted authors—Lewis, Merton, Neuhaus, Sheen, Underhill/pastoral resources/saints—biography, writings/scripture/self-help and healing/spiritual life

OTHER HIGHLIGHTED SECTIONS • current interest/foreign language books/mariology/media studies/philosophy/theology

SERVICES • shipping, special orders

Synod Bookstore

75 E 93 St 10128 (Park-Upper East Side)
369-0288
M-F 10–4, Sat by appointment

Housed within the Synod of Bishops of the Russian Orthodox Church Outside Russia, the small bookshop sells only those books related to the orthodox Christian religion, including histories, biographies, and dogmatic studies.

SERVICES • shipping

Trinity Bookstore
74 Trinity Place 10006 (Broadway-Financial)
602-9689
M-F 9:30–5:30

Just opposite Trinity Church, where services took place for the
first time in 1698 (the original church was destroyed in the
great fire of 1776 and was rebuilt in 1790), is the two-level,
modest, and well-stocked bookstore. New books fill the theological subjects and literature, and, oddly enough, the business
section as well. The manager says there are three types of
customers—those who buy only the business books, those who
buy only the religious titles, and those who buy both. The last
group, he says, are the ones who give him hope.

Ground Floor
MAIN SECTIONS · Bibles/classic literature/common prayer/episcopal
church/select reading/spirituality

OTHER HIGHLIGHTED SECTIONS · new york/poetry/prayer/ref-
erence

Second Floor
MAIN SECTIONS · children's/church history/New Testament—commentaries, survey/Old Testament—commentaries, survey/theology

OTHER HIGHLIGHTED SECTIONS · Christian decision making/com-
parative religions/liturgy/business analysis/banking/bonds/commodities/
fixed income/futures/global/interest rates/investing/money markets/opera-
tions/options/portfolio management/theory/trading/valuation

SERVICES · catalog, shipping, special orders

Trinity Bookstore at the General
Theological Seminary
175 Ninth Ave 10011 (21-Chelsea)
645-1984
M-F 9:30–4:30, Sat 12:30–4:30

The bookstore just off the lobby of the General Theological
Seminary houses a good theology section, with many progres-
sive titles mixed in. The buyer's erudite interests are manifested

in the Other Highlighted Sections, which are not stocked in depth, but provide additional and compelling food for thought.

MAIN SECTIONS • Anglican studies/church history/ethics/management and missiology/New Testament/Old Testament/Old Testament commentaries/pastoral care/reference/spirituality/theology

OTHER HIGHLIGHTED SECTIONS • AIDS/black studies/Christian education/ecumenism/healing/homiletics/Judaica/literature/women's studies

SERVICES • shipping, special orders

Union Theological Seminary Books

3041 Broadway 10027 (121-Morningside Heights)
662-7100
M-F 9:15–4:45, Th –6:30

Union Theological Seminary was built in 1910 in the Gothic tradition of Oxford and Cambridge. The arched way to the bookstore has a wall of windows overlooking the serene interior landscaped courtyard, making it one of the loveliest entries to a bookstore in Manhattan. Once inside, you'll find the store carries a good number of new hardcover and paperback books, notably of a scholarly nature, in many theological categories.

MAIN SECTIONS • black studies/church history/faculty authors/Old and New Testament criticism/pastoral studies/politics/sale books/social ethics/sociology/theology/women's studies

OTHER HIGHLIGHTED SECTIONS • American history/Eastern thought/ecology/education/Native American studies/philosophy

SERVICES • newsletter, shipping, special orders

Unity Center of Practical Christianity Bookstore

213 W 58 St 10019 (Seventh-Midtown)
582-1300
T-W 11–7, Th 11–5, F 11–4

The bookstore at the nonsectarian Unity Center showcases the many works of their minister, Eric Butterworth, who has been practicing in New York for over thirty years. He calls his regular 11:00 A.M. Sunday services at Avery Fisher Hall "an experience of Creative 'Worth-ship.' " Books by other writers on the road of spiritual growth to self-realization, such as Joel Goldsmith, Emmett Fox, and Rollo May, are also stocked in this basement bookstore.

SERVICES · shipping

Also:

The Cathedral Shop
The Cathedral Church
of St. John the Divine
1047 Amsterdam Avenue
New York, New York 10025

Cathedral Shop at St. John the Divine
1047 Amsterdam Ave 10025 (112-Morningside Heights)
222-7200
M-Sun 9–5

Among the splendid reproductions of cathedral ornamentations, kits to build your own cathedral or ark, hand-carved angels and beasts, stuffed animals, and hundreds of additional items for sale, are new books on an array of subjects, including art, literature, psychology, self-help, religion, and the Bible.

Books on Eastern religions can be found in ASIAN and FOREIGN LANGUAGES. For books on Islam see MIDDLE EAST. For books on Judaism see JUDAICA. For stores with books on each of the above and on comparative studies, see NEW AGE.

Civil Service

Civil Service Bookshop
89 Worth St 10013 (Broadway-Financial)
226-9506
M-F 8:30–5

This bookstore carries a general selection of reference titles for civil service and licensing exams, test preparation guides, all Arco Civil Service Review books, and, for those tests not covered by the Arco series, other publishers' examination guides.

SERVICES • shipping

College

Before going to any of the following college bookstores, always call ahead to check their hours; many have shortened summer hours and/or extended hours during the first few weeks of classes.

Baruch College Bookstore
360 Park Ave So 10010 (25-Gramercy)
889-4327
M-Th 9–6, F 9–3

Baruch is a four-year business college selling course books in areas related to business, some computer books, and college test preparation guides.

Borough of Manhattan Community College
199 Chambers St 10007 (West Side Highway-Financial)
608-1023
M-Th 9–7, F 9–5

The bookstore mainly sells course books for this two-year nursing and business school, with a small selection of fiction and horror books.

City College Bookstore
W 138 St & Convent Ave 10031
(West Harlem)
368-4000
M-Th 9–7:30, F 9–3

The bookstore carries all course books for classes given at City College, a four-year liberal arts school within the CUNY system. At the front of the store, amidst magazines, school supplies, and munchies, a good selection of reference books for the student is displayed, as well as a smattering of trade books within the divisions listed below.

MAIN SECTIONS · African American studies/campus authors/*New York Times* bestsellers/reference—career, dictionaries, general, study guides and outlines/sale books

OTHER HIGHLIGHTED SECTIONS · Abrams Discovery Series/anthologies/childcare/children's/computers/gay and lesbian studies/health and fitness/history/Latin American studies/literary theory/literature/new releases/nursing/Penguin Classics/philosophy/political science/psychology/religion/science and ideas/Spanish books/travel—Harvard Student Guides only/women's studies

College of Insurance Bookstore
101 Murray St 10007 (West-Financial)
962-4111
M-F 12–5:30

This store carries only course books for classes given at this four-year insurance and business college.

Collegiate Bookstore at Yeshiva University
2539 Amsterdam Ave 10033 (186-Washington Heights)
923-5782
M-Th 10:30–4:30

The bookstore sells course books for its undergraduate classes and graduate social work school only.

Columbia University Bookstore
2926 Broadway 10027 (115-Morningside Heights)
854-1754
M-F 9–7, Sat & Sun 12–5

The bookstore at this Ivy League school, founded in 1754, carries an extensive stock in several general and academic subjects in addition to the thousands of course books for classes in all undergraduate and graduate schools. It is run by Barnes and Noble, as are many college bookstores around the country, but because of the nature of this prestigious university the book selection far exceeds the usual offering of popular books. All sections contain trade and university presses, in both hardcover and paperback. Books published by Columbia University Press are featured separately, as are books written by campus authors. Of note are the history, philosophy, literary criticism, and sociology sections.

MAIN SECTIONS • American history/ancient history/anthropology/art history/Asian studies/campus authors/Columbia University Press/computers/drama/economics/European history/fiction/gay and lesbian studies/Harvard Loeb Classics/Latin American studies/law reference/linguistics/literary criticism/mathematics/new releases—hardcover, paperback/*New York Times* bestsellers/philosophy/physics/poetry/political science/reference—English and foreign language dictionaries, general, study guides and outlines/science/sociology/Soviet and Eastern European studies/women's studies

OTHER HIGHLIGHTED SECTIONS • Africa and Mideast/architecture/film/media/music/mysteries/mythology and folklore/religion/sale books/Shakespeare/travel

SERVICES • special orders

Fashion Institute of Technology Bookstore
227 W 27 St 10001 (Eighth-Chelsea)
564-4275
M-Th 8:30–7, F 8:30–5, Sat 10–2

Like most other college bookstores, this one also carries magazines, school supplies, sportswear, and stationery, but unlike most others, the books for sale are all related to design, fashion, and the arts. FIT is in the heart of Chelsea's fashion district, and its bookstore carries not only the required course books but a remarkable selection of related books geared toward general retail as well.

MAIN SECTIONS · design/drawing and sketching/fashion/interior design/illustration/photography/sewing and patternmaking/textiles

OTHER HIGHLIGHTED SECTIONS · career reference/Dover/fine arts/jewelry/popular reading—mass market fiction/reference—English and foreign language dictionaries, general

Fordham University Bookstore

113 W 60 St 10023 (Columbus-Midtown West)
636-6000
M-Th 10:30–6:30, F 10:30–4:30

The bookstore at this private university carries course books for its undergraduate and graduate classes exclusively.

Hunter College Bookstore

695 Park Ave 10021 (68-Upper East Side)
650-3970
M-Th 9–7, F 9–4

Course textbooks are primarily available here, with some general trade adult and children's titles mixed in.

Interboro Institute

450 W 56 St 10019 (Tenth-Midtown West)
399-0091

The Interboro Institute is a two-year business college and their bookstore sells course books at the beginning of each semester during the first few weeks of classes only.

John Jay College of Criminal Justice Bookstore

445 W 59 St 10019 (Ninth-Midtown West)
265-3619
M-Th 9–7, F 10–3

Course books only are sold here for classes in criminal justice, crime and police science, and legal philosophy.

New York University Book Center

18 Washington Place 10003 (LaGuardia-Greenwich Village)
998-4654
M-Th 10–7:15, F 10–6, Sat 12–6

The buildings housing New York University are located around Washington Square Park, a public park since 1828, and a potter's field, marsh, public hangings site, and military parade grounds before that. The university consists of fourteen schools, and thousands of course books for classes in each of these schools—including the Tisch School of the Arts, the College of Arts and Sciences, the School of Education, the School of Business, and ten others—can be purchased on the lower level of the Book Center, located just east of the park. The children's book department is here as well as a good selection of books on sale.

On the ground floor, among journals, magazines, sportswear, and school and computer supplies, is the retail trade department of the bookstore, in business over fifty years and offering a wide selection of books in many general and academic areas. Almost all sections contain trade, university, and small presses. The reference selection is exceptional, and of additional note are the fiction and drama sections. Books published by campus authors are featured halfway down the stairs to the textbook department. Be sure to check out the mural of a scene inside a subway station painted by an alumni.

MAIN SECTIONS • anthropology/biography/black studies/business/children's/cookbooks/drama—alphabetical by playwright/drama theory/eco-

nomics/Everyman's Library/faculty publications/fiction/film and media/
history—American and world/Judaica/literary criticism and theory/Loeb
Classics/Modern Library/mysteries/new releases—hardcover, paperback/
New York/philosophy/poetry/politics—American and international/psy-
chology/reference—careers, college guides, English and foreign language
dictionaries, general, study and test preparation guides, writer's/sale books/
sociology/travel—alphabetical by country/women's studies

OTHER HIGHLIGHTED SECTIONS · art—monographs, technique,
theory/astronomy and science/black women writers/education/gay and lesbian studies/health/humor/Latin American studies/linguistics/literary an-
thologies/Mideast studies/music and dance/mythology/nature/photography/
religion/science fiction/sports and games

SERVICES · shipping, special orders

Pace University Bookstore
Pace Plaza 10038 (Spruce-Financial)
349-8580
M-Th 9–7, F 9–5

The bookstore of this four-year school sells only the business
course books required for each class.

Technical Career Institute
320 W 31 St 10001 (Eighth-Midtown West)
594-4000
M-Th 8:45–6:30, F 8:30–4:30

Course books for classes on electronics, refrigeration, ESL,
and office technology are available, as well as reference books
on electronics and air conditioning.

For more course books, also see FASHION—FASHION INSTITUTE OF TECHNOLOGY,
GENERAL—BARNARD BOOKFORUM

Computers

Computer Bookworks
25 Warren St 10007 (Church-Financial)
385-1616
M-Sat 10–6:30

This is the only full-service bookstore in Manhattan offering an extensive selection of titles exclusively related to computers. New books are always discounted 20 percent (for three months), as is one section each month chosen by the manager (except textbooks). Out-of-print computer and textbook titles, business books, and a limited selection of computer supplies are also for sale. Amiable and knowledgeable staff are always online.

MAIN SECTIONS • Computers:
bestsellers/business/communications networking/computer texts/database/
desktop publishing/how-to hardware/IBM and compatible/integrated and
networking/integrated software/language programming/Macintosh/op-
erating systems/professional texts/quick reference guides/spreadsheets/
Unix/windows/word processing
    Business:
accounting/finance/general/international/management/marketing/real es-
tate/reference
    Discounted textbooks include:
chemistry/health/law/medical/miscellaneous/physics

SERVICES • shipping, special orders
Computer Bookworks also runs a BBS, which was down at the time of this
writing but may be accessible now.

The general computer service store located around Manhattan, SOFTWARE ETC. (a division
of Barnes and Noble), also sells computer books. Check the yellow pages listings.

Also, New York University has recently opened

NYU Computer Store
242 Greene St 10003
998-4672
M 10–8, T-F 10–6, Sat 12–6

This store is a full-service shop offering service, repairs, and support in addition to selling hardware, software, supplies, and computer books. Modest selections in various computer-related subjects are available, as are all of the major computer periodicals.

Also see GENERAL—BARNES AND NOBLE, PROFESSIONAL—MCGRAW HILL

Cookbooks

Kitchen Arts and Letters

1435 Lexington Ave 10128
(93-Upper East Side)
876-5550
M 1–6, T-F 10–6:30, Sat 11–6
(call for August hours)

Kitchen Arts and Letters is one of the country's largest stores dedicated to the culinary arts, offering an amazing collection of cookbooks, food and wine guides, and sidelines that include everything but the kitchen sink. Culinary memorabilia such as reproduced tin biscuit boxes, antique food, wine, and crate labels, and early advertising reproductions are for sale among contemporary calendars, stationery, and engagement books all related to food. In addition to the twenty-five hundred plus cookbooks are works about food, including histories, memoirs, essays, and even books on kitchen design. Nahum Waxman, Kitchen's owner and gastronomic specialist, also carries an extensive collection of out-of-print books, and will search for those not in stock, although unusual and rare books on food are plentiful at Kitchen Arts and Letters, as is culinary inspiration for the cook, the gourmet, the professional, and the devourer.

MAIN SECTIONS · American regional cooking/baking and decorating/ cooking literature/cooking and food history/entertaining and party planning/ethnic—everywhere from Aghani to European to Yemenite regional cooking/general/new releases—hardcover, paperback/out-of-prints/professional—chefs, restaurateurs, food preparation/restaurant guides—worldwide/seafood/wines and beverages

OTHER HIGHLIGHTED SECTIONS • antipasto and hors d'oeuvres/
children's cookbooks/breakfast/garnishes/giftbooks/gourmet/grilling/
health/herbs/holiday cooking/macrobiotic cooking/meat/microwave cook-
ing/nutrition/quick cooking/reference/roadside/salads/sauces/seasonal/
soups/vegetarian

SERVICES • o/p searches, shipping, special orders

By appointment only:

Charlotte Safir
1349 Lexington Ave 9-B 10128
534-7933

antiquarian and out-of-print cookbooks

And also:

Anjelica's Herbs and Spices
147 First Ave 10003 (9-East Village)
677-1549
M-Sat 10–7:45, Sun 11–6:45

An in-depth collection on natural foods cooking, nutrition, and
diet books is located at the back of this fresh food market and
dealer in herbs and spices. A wonderful plus to this library is
its division of cookbooks, remedies, and literature related to
specific ailments. Anjelica's is the first name in healthful
reading.

Dean and Deluca
560 Broadway 10012 (Prince-Soho)
431-1691
M-Sat 8–8, Sun 9–7

The rear of this enormous gourmet food store houses an excellent selection of new hardcover and paperback cookbooks as
well as books on sale, out-of-prints, remainders, and imports.
Sections include regional recipes, nutrition, wines, coffees and

teas, and general books on how to cook just about anything. The books and the food are irresistible!

Dance—see DRAMA AND PERFORMING ARTS

Decorative Arts

Archivia

944 Madison Ave 10021
(75-Upper East Side)
439-9194 (fax 744-1626)
M-F 10–6, Sat 11–5

Archivia, a word formed by joining *architecture* and *archives*, is the culmination of combining an in-depth collection of new, imported, rare, and out-of-print books on the decorative arts with a magnificent store design by architect Michael Rubin. The award-winning physical space houses New York's largest selection of volumes related to the decorative arts, architecture, interior design, and gardening. Archivia's owners, Joan Gers and Cynthia Conigliaro, have divided the store into four main sections: architecture and furniture arranged by country, American architecture and furniture, gardening, and the applied arts, including gold, silver, jewelry, textiles, and modern design. Their familiarity with images and designs in these books is as valuable a resource for the decorator and designer as are the books themselves.

SERVICES · catalogs, library purchases, o/p searches, shipping, special orders

Stubbs Books and Prints

153 E 70 St 10021 (Lexingon-Upper East Side)
772-3120 (fax 794-9071)
M-Sat 10–6

Stubbs Books and Prints carries a variety of books on the decorative arts as well as a generous selection of prints related to what the owner describes as "the pleasures of living." Books are either used or out-of-print, many of them being rare and unusual titles, from as early as the seventeenth century, on decorating, design, landscape architecture, and social history, in addition to several on food and wine.

SERVICES • o/p searches, shipping

Opened by appointment only:

Acanthus
48 W 22 St 10010
463-0750

specializes in decorative arts, architecture, and landscape architecture, antique reference books, and interior design

Rick Barandes
41 N. Moore St 10013
941-0826

specializes in books on twentieth-century decorative arts and graphic arts

C. Richard Becker
P.O. Box 20261, London Terrace Station 10011
243-3789

specializes in decorative and fine arts, antique reference books

See listings in ART, ARCHITECTURE, and INTERIOR DESIGN for more booksellers of decorative arts titles, and ADDITIONAL LISTINGS. Dental—see ADDITIONAL LISTINGS and SCIENCE AND MEDICINE.

Dover

Dover Book Store
180 Varick St 9th fl 10014 (Charlton-Greenwich Village)
255-3755
M-F 9–4:30

Dover Publishing Company is a reprint house that publishes (at a very low cost) writings that have entered the realm of public domain. The company has recently started printing original children's and clip-art titles, but the bulk of Dover stock is reprinted works, all in paperback. They even offer a line of literature classics for one dollar each. Their shop is located in the office building housing the publishing company's suite, and it resembles a well-stocked showroom.

MAIN SECTIONS · activity books/antiques/architecture/art/chess/children's/cooking/crafts/fiction/literature/magic and games/music/musical scores/nature/performing arts/photography/science/social sciences

SERVICES · catalog, shipping

Drama and Performing Arts

Applause Theatre and Cinema Books
211 W 71 St 10023 (Broadway-Upper West Side)
496-7511
M-Sat 10–8

Thespians are in heaven at Applause where books on all dramatic genres—theater, film, music and television—are available. The shop is particularly strong in biographies, reference, history, and criticism, and the collection of published paperbound plays, screenplays, and scripts is tremendous. The shelves are stocked with imports and new books, and an expanding collection of out-of-prints. Sidelines include audiotapes, videos, magazines and journals. Applause also publishes its own books on theater and film, all of which are available at the store.

MAIN SECTIONS · acting and directing/American theater/Applause publications/biography—composers, film, theater/costume/film—criticism, history, theory/film—production, editing, language, lighting, directing, sound/film and video guides/monologues/musical and musical comedy history/musical and opera librettos/new releases/play anthologies/plays—by author, international/Samuel French scripts/screenplays/Shakespeare— plays and criticism/stage management and scenery/theater history and criticism/TV and video—production and technique/voice and diction/writing

OTHER HIGHLIGHTED SECTIONS • animation/black theater/children's theater/comedy/fantasy and science fiction/horror/humor/sale books/ television/women playwrights

SERVICES • Applause publications catalogs, shipping, special orders

The Ballet Shop
1887 Broadway 10023 (62-Upper West Side)
678-1654
M-Sat 11–6:30, Sun 12–6:30 (during ballet season only)

Everything for sale at The Ballet Shop is related to dance; even the books on film, theater, and opera speak to the performance aspect within these genres. Although the store is a general gift shop in a small space, the collection of new and out-of-print books is quite good, especially books for children.

MAIN SECTIONS • ballet—individual by title/children's fiction and nonfiction/dancers/history/reference/technique
A small selection of books on film, theater, and opera is also available.

SERVICES • shipping, special orders

Drama Book Shop
723 Seventh Ave 10019
(49-Midtown West)
944-0595 (fax 921-2013)
M-F 9–7 (Wed till 8),
Sat 10–5:30, Sun 12–5

Established in 1923, just seven years after the city's theater district expanded to the Times Square area as the Schuberts began the building of their theaters, the Drama Book Shop remains New York's premiere, most comprehensive source of dramatic arts books.

The selection of individual plays, scripts, and scores is extensive, as are the collections of criticism, theory, and dramatic biography. The sections on other forms of performing arts, including dance, film, and music, are equally remarkable. The computerized inventory consists primarily of new, in print paper and cloth titles all purchased by Drama owners Rozanne and Arthur Seelen. Mr. Seelen, once a member of the 92nd Street Y's Traveling Playhouse for Children, bought the shop over thirty-five years ago and maintains it as the theater society's most animated and resourceful communal greenroom.

MAIN SECTIONS · acting/American and world theater—biography, criticism, history, theory/biography/children's theater/costume—design, handbooks, history/directing/early English—anthologies, biography, criticism, history, plays/film—criticism, general, history, production, technical/ Greek and Roman—anthologies, criticism, history, plays/improvisation/ monologues/music/musical theater—history, libretti, scores/new releases/ play anthologies/play and scriptwriting/plays by title—written in English, translated into English/production and business/sale books/scenes/screenplays by title/set design/Shakespeare—criticism, history, plays/stage management/television and radio—criticism, history, production/theater and education

OTHER HIGHLIGHTED SECTIONS · African American theater/commercials and voiceovers/dance/fundraising/movement and mime/speech and dialects

SERVICES · author signings, readings, and parties, catalogs, shipping, special orders

Samuel French Bookshop

45 W 25 St 2nd fl 10010 (Sixth-Chelsea)
206-8990
M-F 9–5

Samuel French has been a major theatrical publisher since 1830, when they began providing small theater groups throughout the states and into the frontier with published scripts (at that time the only state west of the Mississippi was Missouri). Today they publish several thousand plays, in addition to biographies, autobiographies, theatrical histories, and technical books. Here, in their offices, they also maintain a small bookstore where you can purchase other publisher's titles as well as any Samuel French publication.

MAIN SECTIONS • acting/anthologies/costume/directing/film/librettos/ monologues/plays by author/scenes/technical/theater history/youth productions

OTHER HIGHLIGHTED SECTIONS • getting work/playwriting/ screen writing/speech/stage management

SERVICES • catalog, shipping
Samuel French also maintains an archive of out-of-print plays, and those available in manuscript only, which you can purchase for twenty-five dollars a copy.

Richard Stoddard
18 E 16 St 10003 (Fifth-Chelsea)
645-9576
M T Th Sat 11–6

Richard Stoddard specializes in rare and out-of-print dramatic arts biographies and criticism and specific plays. His collection of old Broadway playbills is outstanding, as are the rare books on costume and scenic design. He also provides a wide range of scholarly and technical titles on theater, dance, and film.

MAIN SUBJECTS • circus/costume design/dance/film/music/opera/plays/ popular entertainment/scenic design/theater

SERVICES • appraisals, catalog, o/p searches, shipping

By appointment only:

Dramatis Personae Booksellers
71 Lexington Ave 10010
679-3705

specializes in books on theater, puppetry, and magic; catalog available

Theatron

250 Fort Washington Ave 2H 10032
923-5814

used and antiquarian books on film and theater

And also:

Actors Heritage

262 W 44 St 10036
944-7490
M-Sat 9:30–11, Sun 11–7

Actor's Heritage is mainly a theater
gift shop with hundreds of sidelines
for sale related to Broadway productions. The sections of new books of-
fer highlights in selected dramatic fields including musical
theater, dance and film, in addition to books on costumes,
monologues, theater history, Stanislavski and technical texts.

For books on film see GENERAL—GOTHAM BOOK MART.

Education

Bank Street College Bookstore

610 W 112 St 10025 (Broadway-Morningside Heights)
678-1654 (fax 316-7026)
M-Th 10–9, F & Sat 10–6, Sun 12–5

Affiliated with the Bank Street College of Education, the bookshop is a two-level store, with new children's books on the
ground level and titles for professionals and parents one flight
up. Wordless board books for babies to paperbacks for young
adult readers fill the street-level shelves, with videos, cassettes,
games, and toys scattered throughout. Upstairs, course books
for students, and titles of interest to parents, students, and
teachers are available. The atmosphere in the store is friendly

and helpful, and the view of the Cathedral of St. John the Divine out of the second floor window is exquisite.

Ground Floor

MAIN SECTIONS • art—general, origami, technique/baby books/beginning readers/concept/fairy tales/fiction—beginning readers to young adult/picture books/poetry/series—Babysitter's Club, Eyewitness, Hardy Boys, Nancy Drew/toddler books

OTHER HIGHLIGHTED SECTIONS • architecture/cookbooks/humor/learning disabilities/music and songbooks/puzzles and games/social issues

Second Floor

art/Bank Street books/curriculum/early childhood/education/folktales and mythology/history and biography/multicultural/music and art/parenting/play/psychology/reading and writing/reference/social studies

OTHER HIGHLIGHTED SECTIONS • anthropology/computers/foreign languages/science

SERVICES • shipping, special orders

Teachers College Bookstore

1224 Amsterdam Ave 10027 (120-Morningside Heights)
678-3920 (fax 678-4048)
M-Th 10–7:30, F 10–5:30, Sat 10–2

Manhattan's prestigious Teachers College prepares more students to enter the field of education than most any other college in the U.S. The large and extensively stocked bookstore serving this university consists of four rooms. At the entrance is the general book room, with many sections containing course books as well as titles for general retail. The education room, the children's room and the stationery and school supplies room follow. Almost any book published by Teacher's College Press can be purchased here, and hundreds of colorful educational aids are displayed and sold throughout the store. However, this resource is not for the teacher and educational student only; children will love it and parents will find it invaluable.

Entrance Room

MAIN SECTIONS • anthropology/biography and autobiography/fiction/history and science/new releases-hardcover, paperback/poetry/psychology/

reference—educational outlines, English and foreign dictionaries, general, study guides/sale books/sociology

OTHER HIGHLIGHTED SECTIONS · African American studies/ AIDS/art/atlases/health/humor/literary essays/New York/philosophy/photography/theater arts

Education Room

MAIN SECTIONS · administration/adult ed/early childhood ed/education/ESL/gifted/higher ed/language/math—computer/measurement/reading/research measurement/special ed/speech pathology and audiology

Children's Room

activity books/art/classroom aids/easy readers/fiction-ages 7 to teens/ folktales/foreign languages/hobbies/language arts/math/multicultural/ mythology/Native Americans/new releases—hardcover, paperback/ nonfiction by subject/picture books/reading/reference/science

SERVICES · shipping, special orders

Erotica

Come Again
353 E 53 St 10022 (First-Midtown East)
308-9394
M-F 11–7:30, Sat 11–6

The extensive selection of books at Come Again (comprised mainly of new paperbacks) includes hundreds of erotica titles for straight men and women and lesbian and gay lovers. Many titles in Grove Press's Victorian Library series are stocked. They also carry a surprising number of how-to books destined to make you Come Again.

SERVICES · catalog (it's on video), shipping

Eve's Garden
119 W 57 St Suite 420 10019 (Sixth-Midtown West)
757-8651
M-Sat 12–6:30 (for women and partners, men can visit alone from 12–2)

Eve's Garden embodies what Aphrodite symbolizes to many women—the idealization of womanhood in all her feminity. This store is dedicated to the celebration of woman and her sexuality. Items for pleasure, body oils, candles, and videos are for sale along with a selection of primarily new paperback books. The main focus of the collection is erotica for women and men, and women and women, in addition to literature on sexual abuse and teenage sex. The staff makes every effort to maximize comfort and privacy while celebrating the pleasures of the garden.

MAIN SECTIONS • erotic stories/lesbian literature/sex abuse/spirituality and tantric sex/sex and teenagers

SERVICES • shipping

For stores carrying more graphic books, you'll have to check the Yellow Pages listings.

Fashion

Design Inspiration
488 Seventh Ave Suite 12C
10018 (36-Midtown West)
736-1537 (fax 736-1537)
M-F 9–6

Marianne Cassone was truly inspired when she opened up Design Inspiration. It's not just a bookstore carrying books on fashion and design—it's an invaluable resource for industry professionals, as the store showcases books related to trends and upcoming seasonal productions. Ms. Cassone constantly watches what new designers are working on, and makes sure her store carries related printed material. She buys books published worldwide, including highly specialized imports. Design Inspiration is the exclusive distributor of books produced by Luigi Brivio of Como, Italy, and Kaigai of Japan. In addition to imported books, numerous fashion, interior design, and graphics magazines from around the world are available here through a subscription service—just one of the many facets of personal service provided by Design Inspiration for artists, buyers, and designers.

MAIN SECTIONS · children's wear/clip-art/color/computer graphics, conversationals/directories/fashion—costumes, designers, history, reference, theater/imports/knitwear/reference/textiles—general, history, instruction, reference

SERVICES · seasonal brochures, shipping, special orders, subscriptions

Fashion Design Books

234 W 27th St 10001 (Seventh-Chelsea)
633-9646 (fax 633-0807)
M-Th 10–5, F 10–3

Located across the street from the Fashion Institute of Technology, Fashion Design Books is a small bookstore carrying some course books for the college as well as a selection of trade books related to various aspects of the fashion industry. Helpful sidelines include art and sewing supplies.

MAIN SECTIONS · anatomy/color/computer arts/design/designers/drawing and sketching/graphic design/history—fashion and costume/jewelry/merchandising/patterns and sewing/photography/reference/textiles—reference

By appointment only:

Gunson and Turner Books

166 E 63 St 10021
826-9381 (fax 980-5736)

specializing in fashion and social history

Check the MUSEUM listings for shops with books on costume.

Foreign Language

Celtic—see IRISH BOOKS

Chinese

All of the following stores are in the heart of Chinatown, home to over 150,000 Chinese.

Elite HK Corporation
5 Bowery 10002 (Pell-Chinatown)
925-4968
M-Sun 10–7

In the back of this stationery-type store that sells greeting cards, writing materials, and a myriad of gift items is a selection of books in Chinese related primarily to Christianity and the Christian way of life. Bibles, concordances, commentaries, studies of the Old and New Testaments, and books on spirituality and Christian living are offered. A variety of Chinese children's books are also for sale, including many that are not on religious topics. A variety of cookbooks, general reference titles, and a good selection of volumes on health and healing are on hand as well.

Jung Ku Books and Stationery
8 Pell St 10013 (Bowery-Lower East Side)
732-1030
M-Sun 10–7

This is a small stationery store with Chinese paperbacks in the rear of the shop. The books include Chinese history and literature, with some reference titles and small selections in other general areas. Chinese newspapers and magazines are also for sale.

Oriental Culture Enterprises, Inc.

13-17 Elizabeth St 2nd fl 10013 (Canal-Chinatown)
226-8461
M-Sun 10–7

This huge and wonderful shop is dedicated to the arts and culture of the Chinese and Chinese-Americans. Music, musical instruments, art prints, art supplies, periodicals, and a phenomenal selection of books in Chinese are housed within this large, bright, colorful space, where many customers appear to spend hours. Subjects within arts and social sciences include but are not limited to art, literature, travel, history, photography, religion, drama, poetry, health, psychology, reference, languages, and cooking. These are stocked with academic and quality titles, with some popular ones as well. Many of the finer art titles are behind glass cases, but the clerks will gladly let you browse through these lovely imported volumes. General sciences, books on Chinese medicine, martial arts, and technical subjects are also here, with a good number of engineering books represented. Fashion, sewing, and design titles are also well stocked.

This inconspicuous second-story shop has only its name printed on a door at street level—presumably a wise move to keep the tourists out. If you cannot read Chinese, the beautiful display of musical instruments and art prints will at least allow a glimpse into Oriental Culture.

SERVICES · shipping, special orders

Yu Lee Bookstore

81–B Bayard St 10013 (Mott-Lower East Side)
349-0451
M-Sun 10:30–8:30

A little bookstore, with newspapers, toys, and posters mixed in, Yu Lee sells primarily popular books in Chinese with a few English texts about China. The volumes are mostly paperbacks.

Dutch—see GERMAN—CARLA HANAUER

French

Les Belles Lettres at the French Institute/ Alliance Française

22 E 60 St 10022 (Madison-Upper East Side)
838-7365
M-Th 11–7, F 11–6

This is the shop for the Francophile. A complete line of French newspapers, magazines, videos, and cards is mixed in among a stock of books completely in French. While the focus is heavy on literature and the arts, the store supplies titles in almost every general subject. If a particular book is not in stock but is in print in France, Les Belles Lettres promises to procure it.

SERVICES • shipping, special orders

Librairie de France

610 Fifth Ave 10020 (49-Midtown West)
581-8810 (fax 475-7658)
M-Sat 10–6:15

In 1934 the late Isaac Molho opened a store that was destined to become a haven for French intellectuals who fled Europe during World War II. Overlooking Rockefeller Center's Channel Gardens, the site was also home to Editions de la Maison Française (founded by Mr. Molho), which published the works of such exiled writers as Saint-Exupery, Maritain, Maurois, and others. Today his son, Emanuel, runs this outstanding bookstore, which provides service to French speakers around the world, through its catalog of almost one hundred thousand titles, and to New York's French and, now, Spanish communities out of a thirty-five-hundred-square-foot site. The store sells French and Spanish adult and children's books in every imaginable category, including books translated into these languages as well as those originally published in them. Sidelines include French and Spanish videos and audio books, plus French newspapers, magazines, posters, films, greeting cards, and games. In addition to this exceptional collection of French and Spanish materials, Mr. Molho amassed the most extensive library of technical, scientific, business, and legal bilingual dictionaries for sale in over one hundred languages. (Cassettes to learn each one of them are also available.) Should you decide to go to Europe to learn firsthand one of the languages represented in this extraordinary store, Librairie de France provides a rental car service through Renault that will save you money on the car, and, as Mr. Molho says with a smile, on a few books as well.

Vivre les livres!

SERVICES • catalog, foreign magazine subscriptions, Renault rental cars, shipping, special orders

By appointment only:

Vieux Livres D'Europe
16 E 65 St 5th fl 10021
861-5694

sells primarily French literature

Also see USED—ARGOSY.

German

Mary S. Rosenberg, Inc.
1841 Broadway 10023 (Columbus-
Upper West Side)
307-7733
M-F 9–5:30

After more than fifty years in bookselling this shop is still going strong even after the recent death of Ms. Rosenberg. Rosenberg, Inc. sells primarily new and out-of-print scholarly books in German, with strong emphasis on literature, history, the arts and sciences, and Germanic culture. Reference books and Judaica titles are also for sale as well as some books in French.

SERVICES • catalog, shipping

By appointment only:

Carla Hanauer
195 Bennett Ave 10040
942-6454

specializes in German history and literature, Dutch history and literature, and Judaica

Peter Tumarkin, Fine Books
310 E 70 St 8M 10021
737-8783 (fax 650-1152)

rare and antiquarian books in and on Germanic languages

See also USED—ARGOSY.

Hebrew

Gurary Israel Trading Company
48 Canal St 10002
(Orchard-Lower East Side)
226-0820
M-F 9–4

Gurary is a wholesaler, importing primarily language and religious texts in Hebrew from Israel, with a few select titles in other subjects. If they have the particular title you're looking for, they will sell retail. You *do* need to have a title in mind as they do not allow browsing in their warehouse.

SERVICES • shipping

Sefer Israel, Inc.

28 W 27 St 402 10001 (Broadway-Chelsea)
725-5890 (fax 689-6534)
M-Th 10–5, F 9–1

Sefer Israel is a major U.S. importer of books from Israel on all aspects of Judaica and the Hebrew language. Every book in this warehouselike space is in Hebrew, and Mr. Gozlan, Sefer's owner, promises that if there's a book you want in Hebrew that is not in stock he will get it for you.

SERVICES · shipping, special orders

For additional books in Hebrew see JUDAICA

Hungarian

Puski-Corvin Hungarian Bookstore

217 E 83 10028
(Third-Upper East Side)
879-8893
M-Sat 9–6:30

New, used, and out-of-print books on almost all aspects of Hungarian culture, political science, history, and literature can be purchased here. Puski-Corvin also sells a good selection of books in English that have been published about Hungary, and Hungarian newspapers.

SERVICES · catalog, shipping

Italian

S. F. Vanni

30 W 12 St 10011
(Fifth-Greenwich Village)
675-6336
MWF 9–6 (closed for lunch 2–3),
TTh 9–1, Sat 9–1

S. F. Vanni is perhaps the only bookstore in this country providing a full range of books in Italian, and has been doing so for over one hundred years. Vanni carries an exceptional collection of general Italian language books as well as academic, reference, and technical titles. Coursebooks in Italian are also available, making up a huge amount of this company's mail order business. For the general reader books range from original literary works in Italian and those translated into this language to classics, art, children's, politics, and folklore. The section on Dante is divine.

SERVICES • shipping, special orders

See also GENERAL—RIZZOLI.

Japanese

Asahiya Bookstores New York Inc.

52 Vanderbilt Ave 10017
(41-Midtown East)
883-0011 (fax 883-1011)
M-Sun 10–8

One of seven stores around the country, Asahiya is a bright, large, full-service Japanese-language bookstore complete with cloth and paperback titles, magazines, Japanese comic books, and a small section of books in English. New release displays include business, economics, literature, history, children's, and parenting, in addition to good selections in the cooking, sports, psychology, reference, and arts sections.

SERVICES • shipping, special orders

Kinokuniya

10 W 49 St 10020
(Fifth-Midtown West)
765-1461
M-Sun 10–7:30

The largest and most in-depth collection of Japanese language books in Manhattan is available at Kinokuniya. New books on every aspect of Japanese life, including literature, art, theater, history, politics, reference, business, and economics are sold, as well as English and American best-sellers that have been translated into Japanese. In addition to books in English written about Japan, Kinokuniya also offers sidelines including language tapes, newspapers, and even comic books.

SERVICES · shipping, special orders

Zen Oriental

521 Fifth Ave 10175 (43-Midtown East)
697-0840 (fax 983-1765)
M-F 10–7, Sat 11–7

Zen Oriental is a well-stocked, spacious store filled with almost nothing but books in Japanese plus newspapers, magazines, and traditional gifts. Some of the books in the literature section, written by Japanese authors, are available and for sale here in English, however the stock and signs are for Japanese speakers. Subjects beside literature include business, history, philosophy, zen, art, health, martial arts, origami, and bonsai.

SERVICES · shipping, Tokyo Family Club

Korean

Koryo Books

35 W 32 St 10001
(Fifth-Midtown West)
564-1844
M-Sat 10–8, Sun 12:30–6:30

Koryo Books is a large, full-service Korean bookstore right in the middle of a block filled with Korean markets, stores, and vendors. Only a handful of books for sale are in English and most of the staff members speak only Korean. Books of a general interest are on the ground level, and technical books are located on the mezzanine. Korean gift items, magazines, and newspapers are also available.

SERVICES • shipping

Mideastern Languages—see MIDDLE EAST

Russian

Victor Kamkin, Inc.

925 Broadway 10010 (21-Chelsea)
673-0776
M-F 9:30–5:30, Sat 10–5

Kamkin is a major U.S. importer of books from Russia and also publishes Russian books. This store is a branch of their main location in Rockville, Maryland, but is quite large and well-stocked with books on every aspect of Russian culture and life. Contemporary and classical literature, history, art, psychology, reference, language, philosophy, religion, music, and science are the subjects offered in addition to a general nonfiction area. Titles are mostly scholarly and technical, with a few popular ones interspersed, which mirrors the quiet and serious ambiance of the store that is broken up periodically by an animated conversation.

SERVICES • shipping

Russian House, Ltd.

253 Fifth Ave 10016 (28 Gramercy)
685-1010 (fax 685-1046)
M-Sat 10–6

Russian House is a large U.S. distributor of Russian books, gifts, and art making its home in a light, gallerylike space, with built-in bookcases filled with works by native authors. The imported books cover a wide range of subjects including art, history, literature, classical works, and the sciences.

SERVICES • catalog, shipping

Spanish

Lectorum

137 W 14 St 10011 (Sixth-Chelsea)
929-2833 (fax 727-3035)
M-Sat 9:30–6:15

Librería Lectorum offers "libros y lectura forjan la cultura," that is, a huge selection of new books in Spanish imported from South America, Spain, and Mexico, ranging from children's, best-sellers, and literature to engineering, computer books, and natural medicine. History and cultural studies are also well represented, as are books translated into Spanish from English. Sections on the literature and history

LIBROS Y
LECTURA
FORJAN LA
CULTURA

LIBRERIA
LECTORUM

of Spain, Mexico, Cuba, Puerto Rico, Columbia, and the Dominican Republic are quite extensive. And rumor has it that Ricardo Montalban has been seen idling in front of the large auto repair section.

SERVICES • shipping, special orders

Librería Moría

628 W 207 St 10034 (Broadway-Harlem)
304-2197
M-Sat 10–7

This small Spanish-language bookstore is uptown in central Harlem. They carry a complete line of books in general subjects with many imports from Mexico and Spain. The stock is mainly paperback, with a good concentration of literature and history.

SERVICES • shipping

Macondo

132 W 14 St (Seventh-Chelsea)
741-3108
M-Sat 10–7

Macondo's owner, a gentleman from Bogotá, sits at a desk in the center of this well-kept bookstore stocked with imports from Mexico, Spain, and South America. The new books are primarily on the arts and literature, although reference and history titles are displayed as well.

MAIN SECTIONS • crítica literaría/diccionarios/historia/literatura española/literatura hispanoamericana/poesía/Puerto Rico/teatro

SERVICES • shipping

By appointment only:

El Cascajero, The Old Spanish Book Mine
506 LaGuardia Pl 10012
254-0905

antiquarian and used Hispanica books; social science and humanities books in Spanish

For additional selections of books in Spanish: FOREIGN LANGUAGE — LIBRAIRIE DE FRANCE, POLITICAL SCIENCE — REVOLUTION, RELIGION — CHRISTIAN PUBLICATIONS.

Ukrainian

Arka
26 First Ave 10009 (1-East Village)
473-3550
M-Sat 10–6

This is a small gift shop with a few shelves of books in the Ukrainian language on the region's history, art, and culture as well as several children's titles. The shop is mostly filled with native crafts, including samples of Ukraine's renowned embroidery.

SERVICES · shipping

Surma Book Co.
11 E 7 St 10003
(Third-East Village)
477-0729
T-Sat 11–6

This wonderful Ukrainian shop has been serving its neighboring Slavic community since 1918, providing clothing, crafts, household objects, periodicals, music, and a large selection of imported books on Ukrainian culture and language. Children's books, history, and literature titles are particularly well-stocked.

MAIN SECTIONS • art and music/biography and autobiography/children's/dictionaries/fiction—classic and contemporary/history/memoirs/miscellaneous/nonfiction/poetry/religion and prayer/Ukrainian language workbooks

SERVICES • shipping

Gardening

While there isn't a bookstore in Manhattan devoted strictly to gardening, there is

The Shop in the Garden
590 Madison Ave 10022 (56-Midtown East)
980-8544
M-Sat 10–6

This is the Manhattan branch of the Bronx Botanical Garden's Gift Shop, appropriately located in the lush IBM atrium. While it is a general gift shop, filled with mugs, cards, seeds, bulbs, baskets, and many other supplies for the green thumb, it also has a good selection of new books. Volumes on how to grow just about anything, photographic essays, guides, reference, landscaping and design books are available.

SERVICES • shipping

The gift shop at the METROPOLITAN MUSEUM OF ART (see p. 159) has a fine selection of general gardening books, and URBAN CENTER BOOKS (see p. 72) has new books on landscape gardening. For rare and out-of-print titles on garden design and landscape architecture, see ARCHIVIA (p. 114) and STUBBS BOOKS AND PRINTS (p. 114). Also, titles on city gardening, general references, and guides are for sale at The Horticultural Society of New York, located at 12 W 58 St, and open Monday through Friday from 10 to 6.

Gay and Lesbian

A Different Light
151 W 19 St 10011 (Seventh-Chelsea)
989-4850
M-Sun 10–midnight

A Different Light is a large and extensively stocked gay and lesbian bookstore of over thirteen thousand titles covering a wide range of subjects, offering over one hundred gay and lesbian magazines in English as well as several foreign languages. Both the gay and lesbian fiction sections are excellent, and there is a wall of gay and lesbian biographies (and friendly notables) that is remarkably exhaustive. Store branches are located in two California cities, and the company periodically publishes a newsletter with writings from all locations. Readings are held here regularly, which is just another reason this less-than-intimate physical space transcends into a true bicoastal community.

MAIN SECTIONS • AIDS/arts/biography/cinema/coming out/feminism/ gay and lesbian studies/history/humor/law/leather/literature—gay and lesbian/mysteries/reference/religion and spirituality/sale books/science fiction

SERVICES • author readings and signings, catalog, poetry series, shipping, special orders

Judith's Room

681 Washington St 10014
(10-West Village)
727-7330
TWTh 12–8, F & Sat 12–9, Sun 12–7

Judith's Room is Manhattan's only feminist bookstore, stocking new books by women and about women as well as books on issues central to women in general and lesbians in particular. Contemporary and classic titles by women stock the fiction, mystery, and science fiction sections, with nonfiction sections stocked primarily, but not exclusively, with works by women. The store is conducive to browsing and reading (several chairs and a couch are provided), and to conversing. Staff people are friendly and know their stock.

MAIN SECTIONS • biography/children's/fiction/health/history/lesbian fiction/lesbian poetry/poetry/science fiction and mysteries/spirituality/ women of color/women's studies

OTHER HIGHLIGHTED SECTIONS • body politics/cooking/Judaica/ literary criticism/nutrition/parenting/psychology/reference/sale books/ travel

SERVICES • author readings and signings, catalog, discussion groups, shipping

Oscar Wilde Memorial Bookshop

15 Christopher St 10014 (Sixth-Greenwich Village)
255-8097
M-Sun 11–7:30

Founded in 1967, this is the world's first bookstore for the gay and lesbian community. Its logo bears a labyris superimposed over a pink triangle in expression of both lesbian pride and gay resistance. The small and well-stocked shop is equally divided between lesbian and gay male literature, mostly in paperback, although new hardcovers are displayed in the center racks. Many small and alternative presses are available, alongside gay and lesbian periodicals. The staff is very friendly and pride is far from a sin here.

Both the gay and lesbian sections are divided into these main topics:

> biography/children's/coming out/drama/erotica/fiction/health and counseling/humor/parenting/plays and theater/poetry/relationships/spirituality/theory and criticism—cultural and literary

There are also sections on men and women of color, travel guides, and AIDS.

SERVICES • catalog, shipping, special orders

To receive a catalog of new and out-of-print books related to gay libera-tion, men's issues, and male homosexuality, write to Paths Untrodden, P.O. Box 3245, Grand Central Station 10163, or call 661-5997 to re-quest one.

Also see GENERAL—THREE LIVES AND CO.

Hobbies

America's Hobby Center
146 W 22 St 10011 (Sixth-Chelsea)
M-F 9–5:30, Sat 9–3:30

This large hobby center has a selection of books on model trains, airplanes, boats, radio-controlled toys, and general hobbies.

Horses

Although there isn't a bookstore devoted completely to horses, this equestrian company's book department sits tall in the saddle:

H. Kauffman and Sons
419 Park Ave South 10016 (29-Gramercy)
684-6060
M-Sat 9:30–6:30, Sun 12–5

No horsing around here—these are serious books on training, stable management, dressage, riding competition, breeds, and horse care, in addition to many fiction and nonfiction titles for young riders.

SERVICES • shipping

Humor

By appointment only:

Book Chest
322 W 57 St 34S 10019
246-8955

specializing in rare and antiquarian books on humor, carica-
ture, and satire from the fifteenth to the twentieth centuries

Interior Design

Morton Interior Design Bookshop
989 Third Ave 10022 (59-Midtown East)
421-9025
M-Sat 11–8, F 11–6

On busy Third Avenue the Morton Interior Design Bookshop
is one small square room of strictly faced-out, oversize, hardcover coffee-table books. Subjects covered are architecture,
interior design, gardening, and decoration.

SERVICES · shipping ($200 minimum)

For more books on interior design see DECORATIVE ARTS

International and National Affairs

United Nations Bookstore
General Assembly Building 10017
(46 & First-Midtown East)
963-7680
M-Sun 9–5

United Nations
Bookstore

Although the United Nations welcomes almost two thousand
international visitors daily, and uses six languages officially, the

bookstore's stock is predominantly filled with books in English, although some Spanish and French translations are on display. Every official U.N. publication, and those produced by its related agencies, are for sale. A few general trade titles are mixed in among these bureaucratic texts.

MAIN SECTIONS • agriculture/children's/country studies/development/ economics/education/energy/environment/health/human rights/industry and trade/international law/language books/peace studies/population/reference and dictionaries/statistics/travel/United Nations/United Nations publications/women's studies

OTHER HIGHLIGHTED SECTIONS • art/bargain books/cookbooks

SERVICES • catalog of U.N. publications, shipping

U.S. Government Printing Office Bookstore

26 Federal Plaza Fed Bldg Rm 110 10278 (Broadway-Financial)
264-3825 (fax 264-9318)
M-F 9:30–4:30

You'll have to go through a security checkpoint, but once inside you'll be in the midst of our nation's publications of inexpensive books and pamphlets on history, statistics, and laws as well as guidebooks, references, and government recommendations. You can buy copies of Supreme Court decisions, federal regulatory codes, hazardous waste reports, budget studies, family laws, and international agreements. Best-sellers available include *Columbus's Voyages, First Lunar Landing as Told by the Astronauts*, the government's catalog of recommended books for children, and the documented *American Military History*. Several hundred government periodicals are also available through a subscription service offered here.

MAIN SECTIONS • agriculture/business and industry/careers/children and family/computers/consumer aids/education/energy/environment and weather/government/health/history/hobbies/housing/international topics/ law/military/national topics/science and technology/space exploration/transportation/travel and vacation

SERVICES • catalog, shipping

Irish

Irish Books

580 Broadway Rm 1103 10012 (Houston-Soho)
274-1923
M-F 11–5, Sat 1–4

According to George Moore, Irishmen had to leave Ireland to be heard; if that's still true, here's the sounding board for New York's Irish community. Proprietor Angela Carter (no, not the recently deceased author) runs this small store wherein you can explore the riches of Ireland's art, history, literature, and mythology. Carter maintains the shop as a resource center for the city's Irish population and regularly distributes a catalog listing new books both in the English and Irish languages, events around town, and miscellaneous relevant information. Irish Books has published *A Reader's Guide to Books in the Irish Language*, written by Seosamh McCloskey, which is for sale at the shop in addition to hundreds more new and used titles about Ireland and the history of its people in and away from their homeland.

MAIN SECTIONS · Celtic art and design/Celtic language books/children's/drama/geneology/history/Irish in America/Joyce/law, sociology, and economy/literary criticism/literature/mythology/Northern Ireland/poetry/sale books/travel/women's studies

SERVICES · catalog, shipping, special orders

Judaica

Jewish Book Center of the Workmen's Circle/Arbeter Ring

45 E 33 St 10016
(Park-Midtown East)
889-6800 ext 285
M-Th 9–6, F 9–4:30, Sun 11–3

The Workmen's Circle is a national Jewish fraternal organization dedicated to the maintenance of Jewish identity. Cultural activities, programs for the vitalization of Yiddish culture in the U.S. and abroad, and programs for social and economic justice, as well as for children's and adult education, are sponsored by the circle for members around the country. The small bookshop located in their national headquarters provides a modest selection of English and Yiddish books in several subjects related to Jewish culture. The Arbeter Ring also publishes many Judaica titles that can be purchased here.

MAIN SECTIONS • biography/children's/cookbooks/history/Holocaust/ literature/religion/sale books/song books/Yiddish study guides

OTHER HIGHLIGHTED SECTIONS • folklore/humor/women's studies

SERVICES • catalog, shipping

Judaica Emporium
3070 Broadway 10027
(121-Morningside Heights)
662-7000
M-Th 10–6:30, F 10–2:30, Sun 11–4

Judaica Emporium is a modest-sized shop selling books in a variety of subjects related to Jewish life and culture. Many of the books are new, but the store does carry a good selection of rare and out-of-print titles. The books in the Hebrew and Yiddish literature sections are both new and used.

MAIN SECTIONS • Bible texts and studies/dictionaries/Hebrew language and instruction/Hebrew literature/history/Holocaust/Jewish authors/Jewish law/Judaica/literature/liturgy/midrash/out-of-prints/philosophy/sale books/ Talmudic texts and studies/Yiddish literature/women's studies

OTHER HIGHLIGHTED SECTIONS • biography/cookbooks/Kabbalah/Maimonides/mysticism

Judaica Experience

208 W 72 St 10023
(Broadway-Upper West Side)
724-2424
M-Th 10–7:30, F 10–3, Sun 10–6

This spacious, three-room, second-story shop is filled with books, gifts, music tapes, and Jewish religious items. Their selection of new titles in the bright front room covers the subjects listed below, with a modest number of titles running the gamut from popular to scholarly. In the rear of the store is a children's room that is more like a child's playroom—replete with toys and books, and indestructibly decorated.

MAIN SECTIONS · Bibles/children's—Hebrew and English/contemporary Judaism/cookbooks/family/Hebrew grammar and language/history/Holocaust/holy days/Kabbalah/literature/photography/prayer books/reference/Talmud/women in Judaism/young adult—fiction and nonfiction

SERVICES · shipping, special orders

J. Levine Religious Supplies

5 W 30 St 10001 (Fifth-Chelsea)
695-6888
M-W 9–6, Th 9–7, F 9–2, Sun 10–5

J. Levine, in business since 1820, is a large, two-story shop selling an incredible array of Judaica items. Beautiful seder plates and menorahs are downstairs, among many other items, and upstairs, in the back half of the store, is Levine's comprehensive book collection. Hardcover traditional religious texts in Hebrew are available alongside popular Jewish paperback literature and oversize photography books. The depth of material ranges from titles on the Holocaust to the latest by Alan Dershowitz. Reference books, dictionaries, prayer books, and Bibles are well-stocked, and the staff is well known for their friendly service and in-depth knowledge.

MAIN SECTIONS · children's/ethics/gift books/Halacha/history/Holocaust/introduction to Judaism/Israel/literature/liturgy/philosophy/photography/psychology/reference/Shabbat/women's/Yiddish

OTHER HIGHLIGHTED SECTIONS • art/archeology/Bibles/biography/cookbooks/family/genealogy/Hebrew books and primers/kashrut/midrash/mishnah/prayer books/reference/Talmud

SERVICES • shipping, special orders

Stavsky Hebrew Bookstore
147 Essex St 10002 (Rivington-Lower East Side)
674-1289
Sun-Th 9:30–5

Religious supplies and items of all kinds that pertain to Jewish life fill this large store that stocks general works. Books are divided into religious and educational texts, children's, history, literature, and the sciences, with most of the works in English, although many imported books in Hebrew are also available. Israeli and Yiddish music is for sale along with beautiful cantorial recordings.

SERVICES • shipping

Westside Judaica
2412 Broadway 10024 (88-Upper West Side)
362-7846 (fax 787-4202)
M-Th 10:30–7, F 10:30–3,
Sun 10:30–5

This large store carries a full line of religious articles, gifts, and toys, and along the shop's sides are its new books. One long wall holds fiction and nonfiction titles in both paper and hardcover of general Jewish interest, while religious texts are on the opposite wall. Titles are for sale in Hebrew and English and cover virtually all aspects of Jewish life and culture.

MAIN SECTIONS • biography/children's/cookbooks/Hebrew texts/history/Holocaust/holy days/Israel and diaspora/Jewish culture/Jews in America/Judaism/literature/poetry/rabbinical texts/Talmudic studies/Torah/worship

SERVICES • shipping, special orders

World Zionist Organization Bookstore
110 E 59 St 4th fl 10022 (Park-Midtown East)
339-6000
M-Th 9–5, F 9–1

Publications of the World Zionist Organization, imported
from Jerusalem, are for sale in this tiny store within an office.
The focus is on educational and cultural studies, with an emphasis on Torah and Talmudic texts. Herzl publications, English titles on Zionism and Israel, are also obtainable here, as
well as a limited number of children's books. Overall there are
only a few hundred volumes available, which is about equal to
the number of questions the guard will ask you before you're
allowed admittance. Security is tight.

SERVICES · shipping

Open by appointment only:

Aurora Fine Books
547 W 27 St Suite 570 10001
947-0422 (fax 947-0422)

specializing in used and out-of-print books in Judaica, art
(Jewish as well as American and European), and German

M. Landy Fine Judaica
19 E 71 St 10021
628-2034 (fax 628-8276)

rare books on Judaica and Hebraica

Evelyn Pearl
219 W 81 St #5A 10024
877-1704

rare and out-of-print titles in Judaica, in addition to general
stock and children's books

Also see HEBREW and ADDITIONAL LISTINGS; for books on Judaism and Kabbalah
see NEW AGE.

Law

Lawbook Exchange, Ltd.
135 W 29 St 10001 (Sixth-Chelsea)
594-4341
M-F 9–5

Located in an office building, this shop specializes in sets of law-related subjects, such as statutes, laws, regulations, etc., that are primarily for the professional. They also stock many scholarly antiquarian volumes on constitutional law, legal history, crime, and Americana.

SERVICES • catalog, shipping

MJ and K Books
55 Fifth Ave 10003
(13-Greenwich Village)
790-0339
MTTh 10:30–3:30, W 9:30–11:30

This small bookstore carries law books required for the Cardozo School of Law, plus the following study guides: Casenotes, Emanuel, Gilbert, Legalines, and Smith's.

New York Law School Books
47 Worth St 10013
(W Broadway-Financial)
431-2315
M & T 11–7, W & Th 9–9, F 9–7

The bookstore at this downtown law school carries only the law texts, casebooks, and hornbooks required for classes. In addition to supplies, law flashcards and charts, the following study outlines are also available: Blond's, Emanuel, Gilbert, Law-in-a-Flash, and Nutshell.

SERVICES • shipping

Universal Law Book Co., Inc.

225 Broadway Lower Level B 10007
(Barclay-Financial)
227-0163
M-F 9–5

The door of this basement shop opens into what looks like a miniature law library. Four long walls of shelving around the store are filled with almost every in print law text, casebook, hornbook, and treatise arranged alphabetically by author's name. A few desks and tables are placed in the center of the shop amidst more bookcases, these filled with the law-related subjects listed below, stocking not only professional texts and outlines but some popular trade titles as well. Charts, study guides, flashcards, and practitioner's pamphlets are also available. And two prints of Abraham Lincoln oversee it all.

MAIN SECTIONS · law texts, casebooks, hornbooks, statutes, and treatises arranged alphabetically by author/American law history/Constitution and First Amendment/internal revenue and taxation/legal research and writing/litigation and trial/law practice/New York law/product liability/reference/Supreme Court

Series include Black, Blond's, Emanuel, Gilbert, Nutshell, NYSBA.

SERVICES · shipping, special orders.

Also see PROFESSIONAL—NYU PROFESSIONAL BOOKSTORE

Lexicography

By appointment only:

Madeline Kripke Books

317 W 11 St 10014
989-6832

premier specialist in antiquarian dictionaries, grammars, books on language

Also see REFERENCE

Literature and Modern First Editions

Lorraine Wilbur's Gramercy Book Shop

22 E 17 St Rm 1625 10003 (Union Sq W-Chelsea)
255-5568
M-F 11–4

This little known and well-hidden two-room shop on the six-teenth floor of an office building in Union Square houses an excellent selection of literature written in English. The space may not be huge, but the selection is vast because of Ms. Wilbur's knowledge (she's been a bookseller for over thirty years) and the fact that behind every row of books is another row. The entrance room is filled with seventeenth-, eighteenth-, and nineteenth-century English literature. The slightly larger room to the left houses an extensive selection of twentieth-century American literature. Some are rare volumes or first editions, while others are hard-to-find used hardcovers at excellent prices. Be prepared to spend more time than originally planned.

The following general and used bookshops are well known for their selection of modern first editions: ARGOSY (see p. 42), GOTHAM (see p. 25), PAGEANT (see p. 53), SKYLINE (see p. 55), and STRAND (see p. 56).

By Appointment Only:

William Alatriste

10 Downing St 10014
366-0604

eighteenth-century English and American literature

Ampersand Books

P.O. Box 674 Cooper Station 10003
674-6795

modern first editions of American writers only

Brazen Head Books

235 E 84 St 10028
879-9830

modern first editions in English and in translation

G. Curwen, Books

1 W 67 St #710 10023
595-5904

modern firsts, detective fiction, some performing arts

Firsts and Company

25 E 83 St 10028
249-4122

modern first editions

Glenn Horowitz

141 E 44 St #808 10017
557-1381

modern first editions

David Johnson, Fine and Rare Books

360 E 65 St 4G 10021
879-1853

first editions of English and American literature

Isaac Mendoza Book Company

77 W 85 St 6-F 10024
362-1129

modern first editions, mystery, and science fiction

Nudel Books
135 Spring St 10012
966-5624

modern first editions, rare black literature and poetry

Paulette Rose, Fine and Rare Books
360 E 72 St 10021
861-5607 (fax 861-5619)

American, English, and French literature by and about women; women in literature

See listings under ANTIQUARIAN
Medicine—see SCIENCE AND MEDICINE

Middle East

Pak Books
137 E 27 St 10010 (Lexington-Gramercy)
213-2177
W–Sat 11–6:30

Pak carries new and used books, journals, and magazines on the culture and civilization of Islam and the Middle East in English and foreign languages. History, religion, children's, and language texts are well stocked, along with imports from the Middle East and France. The store has limited retail hours, but will also open by appointment, in sha-Allah.

MAIN SECTIONS • Arabic/art and calligraphy/children's/doctrine and culture/economics/Farsi/Fiqh/Hadith/history/Irfan/Islam/languages/literature/prayer/Qur'an/sale books/sociology/Sufism/references and dictionaries/Tafsir/travel/Urdu

OTHER HIGHLIGHTED SECTIONS • biography/cooking/French/Malcolm X/Spanish/women and family

SERVICES • catalog, shipping

Camel Book Company

P.O. Box 1936 Cathedral Station 10025
865-4093

The Camel Book Company sells used and rare books on Islam by mail only, although you may call them to inquire about a title or to request one of their regularly issued catalogs. Books on the Middle East, North Africa, and Judaica are also available.

To request a catalog of prayer books and illustrated texts call Fil Caravan at 421-5972.

For books on the religions of the Middle East see SUFISM and NEW AGE.

Military and Aviation

Military Bookman

29 E 93 St 10128 (Madison-
Upper East Side)
348-1280
T-Sat 10:30–5:30

As you step down and enter the Military Bookman, located just below street level in one of the many elegant townhouses found on the Upper East Side, you may be a bit disarmed to find such a complete and extensive selection of books on the history of wars in such a warm, inviting, home-like atmosphere. The shop winds through several rooms with well-organized shelves, prints, and original war art displayed on brick walls, and the occasional easy chair. On the shelves (arranged chronologically) are thousands of rare, used, and out-of-print titles covering the military, naval, and aviation histories of virtually every country and every period.

MAIN SECTIONS · Americana—Civil War, colonial, and revolution, western frontier/aviation/British Army—Africa and small wars, general,

India/espionage—post-1945/naval Americana—revolution and nineteenth-century/Poland and Polish forces—all periods/Russian Revolution/Spanish Civil War/tanks and armored operations/World War I—eastern front, general, home front/World War II—Nazi Germany and Fascism, pacific theater

SERVICES • catalog, o/p searches, shipping

Sky Books International
48 E 50 2nd fl 10022
(Park-Midtown East)
688-5086
M-Sat 10–7

Sky Books International probably has the world's largest collection of new books on aviation and military history. A former RAF instructor began it as a mail order business, but it soon took off, and now the public is welcome to peruse the books and periodicals arranged by air, land, and sea (that is, aviation, ground, and naval warfare). Within these three subdivisions the books are arranged chronologically, with good collections of history, biography, and technical titles. This is *the* layover for the flight enthusiast.

SERVICES • shipping, special orders

And by appointment only:

Peter Hlinka Historical Americana
P.O. Box 310 10028
409-6407

specializing in used and rare books on Americana warfare and military history

Also, The Compleat Strategist sells games and hobby items on war and strategy, with a modest selection of related books on warfare, war games, science fiction, and fantasy. The store is located at 11 E 33 Street, just off Fifth Avenue, or call them at 685-3880.

Museums

American Craft Museum
40 W 53 St 10019
(Fifth-Midtown West)
956-3535
T 10–8, W-Sun 10–5

The museum is dedicated to the collection and exhibition of twentieth-century American craft in mediums including clay, wood, fiber, metal, glass, and other exotic materials. The gift shop, an open space at the entrance, has a very small selection of books on general crafts, wood, ceramics, fiber, glass, and jewelry in addition to handsomely produced catalogs of present and past exhibitions.

American Museum of Natural History Shop
79 & Central Park W 10024
(Upper West Side)
769-5150
Sun-Th 10–5:30, F & Sat 10–7:30

The museum shop carries a small selection of new books in subjects that include earth science, natural history, Native American people, anthropology, Eskimos, animals, ocean life, archeology, and field guides. A variety of children's books are stocked in these subjects as well. Needless to say, the more extensive topics covered are dinosaurs and astronomy.

SERVICES · shipping

Children's Museum of Manhattan
212 W 83 St 10024
(Amsterdam-Upper West Side)
721-1223
MWTh 1:30–5:30, F Sat Sun 10–5

Nonfiction and educational activity books are the focus of the selection in the small shop at the Children's Museum of Manhattan. Subjects include art, science, nature, drama, journalism, and the brain. (You don't have to be a kid to enjoy the Brainatarium and Magical Patterns.) And, if you or your child would rather make a book than buy one, you can do so in the Art Studio.

Cooper Hewitt Museum Shop
2 E 91 St 10128 (Fifth-Upper East Side)
860-6939 (fax 860-6909)
T 10–9, W-Sat 10–5, Sun 12–5

Housed in a mansion constructed for Andrew Carnegie in 1901, the Cooper Hewitt Museum is the Smithsonian Institution's National Museum of Design, holding approximately thirty thousand prints and drawings (some as old as three thousand years) primarily related to ornament, design, and architecture. The museum shop is located in just another room of what Carnegie described as "the most modest, plainest, and roomiest house in New York."

MAIN SECTIONS • architecture/children's/Cooper Hewitt publications/ decorative arts/furniture/gardening/gift books/graphic design/historical design/jewelry/New York/textiles

Fraunces Tavern Museum Store
54 Pearl St 10004 (Broadway-Financial)
425-1778
M-F 10–4:45, Sat 12–4

On December 4, 1783, George Washington bid farewell to his officers here at Samuel Fraunces's tavern, a Georgian brick building constructed in 1719. The store carries a small selection of new books on Washington, in addition to books on decorative arts and paintings from the eighteenth and nineteenth centuries, early American history, and books related to current exhibitions.

SERVICES • shipping

Solomon Guggenheim Museum Bookstore
1071 Fifth Ave 10128 (88th-Upper East Side)
727-6200
F-W 10–8, Th 11–6 (however, museum is closed on Thursdays)

The Guggenheim Museum is modern art inside and out. The bookstore carries a fine selection of books on its architect, Frank Lloyd Wright (the Guggenheim is Wright's sole New York City building), in addition to a considerable number of modern artists' monographs.

MAIN SECTIONS · architecture and design/children's/exhibition catalogs/museum publications/publications on artists/reference/Frank Lloyd Wright

SERVICES · shipping

Branch

Guggenheim Museum Soho
575 Broadway 10012 (Prince-Soho)
Sun-W 11–6, Th-Sat 11–10

Jewish Museum Bookshop
1109 Fifth Ave 10128 (92d-Upper East Side)
423-3269
Sun, MWTh 11–5:45, Tues 11–8

The most extensive collection of Judaica can be found in the Jewish Museum, housed in the former Warburg mansion built by Charles Gilbert in 1908. Works by Jewish writers, artists, and thinkers as well as historical and other nonfiction texts are among the new books for sale at the shop, along with a selection of general gifts (of note are the exquisite bookmarks designed by W. Turnowsky and imported from Tel Aviv).

MAIN SECTIONS · American Jews/artists/children's and young adult/exhibition catalogs/fiction/gift books/Holocaust/reference/religion and philosophy/Sephardic histories

OTHER HIGHLIGHTED SECTIONS · biography/cookbooks/film and music/holidays/women's studies

SERVICES · shipping

Metropolitan Museum of Art Bookshop
1000 Fifth Ave 10028 (82-Upper East Side)
879-5500 ext 2911
T-Th 9:30–5:15, F & Sat 9:30–8:45,
Sun 9:30–5:15

Frederick Law Olmsted, Central Park's designer, regretted permitting construction of the museum along the northeastern section of the park. At that time, in 1870, the museum's collection numbered approximately 170 paintings. Today, over 3.25 million works of art housed in almost 1.5 million feet of floor space reach far beyond the space Olmsted originally conceded.

The museum's two-level gift shop is probably more the size Olmsted had in mind. Jewelry, ties, scarves, rugs, art reproductions, sculptures, china, children's gifts and toys are for sale, but most remarkable is the huge book selection. New books of every kind are stocked—paperbacks, hardcovers, oversize tomes, popular and scholarly titles. Every subject contains historical, theoretical, and biographical works, and the selection of monographs is astounding. All of the museum's own publications are available here, in addition to an extensive selection of exhibition catalogs. And if these aren't treasures enough, gallery 6 in the museum's Islamic art wing has on display exquisite pages from fifteenth-century illuminated manuscripts that should keep you here a few more hours.

MAIN SECTIONS • African art/American art/architecture/art of the Americas/Asian art/costume/decorative arts—American, European, general/Egyptian art/European paintings and drawings/gardening and nature/general art/Greek and Roman art/impressionism/Islamic art/medieval art and history/MMA exhibition catalogs, guides, publications/photography/sale books/twentieth-century art

OTHER HIGHLIGHTED SECTIONS • ancient Near East/arms and armor/art of the Pacific/Dover reprints/furniture/music/New York/origami/prints/quilts/travel/women's studies/Frank Lloyd Wright

SERVICES • catalog, shipping

Museum of American Folk Art

61 W 62 St 10023 (Broadway-Upper West Side)
977-7170
M-F 10:30–5:30

A small selection of books on American folk art from the eighteenth century to the present is available at the gift shop of this museum, which holds approximately half a dozen exhibitions per year on such topics as Shaker furnishings, gravestone rubbings, paintings, and toys and dolls. General folk art history and biographies as well as volumes on particular crafts are available.

ᴛʜᴇMUSEUM STORES
The Museum of Modern Art, New York

Museum of Modern Art Store

11 W 53 St 10019 (Fifth-Midtown West)
708-9700
Sat-Tues 11–6, Th & F 12–8:30

MoMA's bookstore has an excellent selection of new books on modern art and artists and an equally remarkable collection of art theory and cultural criticism titles. Other categories include film, photography, architecture and design, art history, and reference. All of MoMA's own publications are also available here. You can spend time looking through your purchases in MoMA's sculpture garden of works by Rodin, Picasso, Miro and others.

SERVICES · shipping

Museum of the City of New York Shop

1220 Fifth Ave 10029 (103-Upper East Side)
534-1672
W-Sat 10–5, Sun 1–5

The museum inside this five-floor red brick building was founded in 1923 to allow New Yorkers to become acquainted with their city's history. Dutch influence and presence, great fires, early New Yorkers, communications, art, and John D. Rockefeller are among the subjects highlighted in the various exhibitions. The small gift shop has a selection of books related to these topics as well as adult and children's titles on general New York City history.

SERVICES • shipping

National Museum of the American Indian
155 St & Broadway 10032
283-2420
T-Sat 10–4:30, Sun 1–4:30

The gift shop at this museum celebrating the life and culture of Indians from both North and South America includes a wonderful selection of books for adults and children. Native American histories, fables, and stories are available for younger readers, while books for adults include titles in history, lore, and arts and crafts. (The museum plans to move just before publication of this book—please call for their new address.)

New-York Historical Society Museum Shop
170 Central Park W 10024 (76-Upper West Side)
873-3400
M-F 10–5

A small selection of books related to New York City and State and their histories, plus some books on Americana are for sale in this elegant museum that houses all but two of Audubon's original drawings for "Birds of America." All of the society's own publications are available here as well.

Pierpont Morgan Library
29 E 36 St 10016 (Park-Midtown East)
685-0008
T-Sat 10:30–5, Sun 1–5

J. P. Morgan seriously collected books, manuscripts, and drawings for over twenty years, amassing an impressive collection of illuminated manuscripts and books in fine binding in addition to musical and literary autographed manuscripts. Books in any way related to the library's collection are for sale in the gift shop, where toys, cards, and gift items are also available. In the library, preserved as it was when Morgan died in 1913, is a hidden stairway behind the bookcases with volumes that will keep you mesmerized for hours.

SERVICES · catalog, shipping

Studio Museum in Harlem Bookshop
144 W 125 St 10027 (Lenox-Harlem)
864-1500
W-F 10–5, Sat & Sun 1–6

The Studio Museum in Harlem regularly features changing exhibitions of black culture and art from Africa, the Americas, and the Caribbean, in addition to their permanent collection, which includes the works of such artists as Romare Bearden and James Van DerZee. A good selection of books related to black culture and art, including biographies and histories, are available here.

Whitney Museum of American Art
945 Madison Ave 10021 (75-Upper East Side)
570-3614
T 11–8, W-Sat 11–6, Sun 12–6

The Bauhaus's Marcel Breuer designed this gray granite structure, which houses an eight thousand-piece permanent collection of American art. In its gift shop is a selection of books related primarily to twentieth-century art, including biographies, monographs, theory, and history. Also available are catalogs of current and past exhibitions.

SERVICES • shipping

Music

Brown's Music Co.

61 W 62 St 10023 (Columbus-Upper West Side)
541-6236
M-Sat 10–7, Sun 12–6

Brown's sells a small selection of books on instruments, musical biographies and history, music appreciation, and opera scores. The bulk of their stock consists of songbooks and sheet music.

Joseph Patelson Music House

160 W 56 St 10019
(Seventh-Midtown West)
582-5840
M-Sat 9–6

In 1891 Carnegie Hall opened its doors, and since then such great musicians as Tchaikovsky, Mahler, Walter, Toscanini, Bernstein, Basie, Ellington, and of course, Billie Holiday, have walked in. Behind the hall is Patelson's Music House, where maestros and musicians—from great to amateur—have been coming in since 1920. Patelson's houses the world's widest selection of scores, sheet music, and librettos and the city's finest collection of music books. The selection of new hardcovers and paperbacks includes scholarly presses, imported books, texts, and quality trade titles. Each musical genre contains history, theory, references, and biographies. The staff is very helpful and will order what's not on the shelves.

MAIN SECTIONS · biography/dictionaries/guides/international songs/ music appreciation and history/musicals and show tunes/opera/reference/ singers/singing and voice/theory

SERVICES · shipping, special orders

By appointment only:

Wurlitzer Brück
60 Riverside Dr 10024
787-6431 (fax 496-6525

specializing in music, books on music, related art, and ephemera

At New York's Lincoln Center, 62d Street and Columbus Avenue, there are three shops carrying a wide range of books in various performance fields. The gift shop at the METROPOLITAN OPERA HOUSE *carries opera librettos, histories, biographies, and reference books. The book store at the* JUILLIARD SCHOOL OF MUSIC *has an extensive selection of books on music, including biography, reference, history, and musical scores. The* PERFORMING ARTS GIFT SHOP *has books for children on dance and opera, as well as the classics and Mozart.*

Also:

See Hear
59 E 7 St 10003 (First-East Village)
982-6968
M-Sun 12–8

See Hear is mainly a music periodicals and magazine wholesaler, with a concentration in rock and some jazz and blues on the side. They do have a selection of books on each of these musical forms.

Fanzines, Magazines, & Books.

See Hear
59 East 7th Street
New York, NY 10003
212-505-9781
Store Hours: 12-8, 7 Days
Mail Order & Wholesale
212-982-6968
Send $2.00 ($3.00 outside U.S.A.)
for our mail order catalog

To receive a catalog of books on early music (including biographies, history, and instruction), call Courtly Music at 580-7234. For stores stocking more music books than books on musical subjects, see

Binzer Music House
218 E 81 St
737-1146
M-Th 11–6, F & Sat 11–5

Carl Fischer Music Store
56–62 Cooper Square
777-0900
M-Sat 10–5:45

Colony, Inc.
1619 Broadway
265-2050
M-Sun 10–Midnight

Mystery

Foul Play
10 Eighth Ave 10014
(12-West Village)
675-5115
M-Sat 11–9:45, Sun 11–7

Renoir said it took him forty years to discover that the queen of all colors is black. This Monarch of Darkness has reigned in Foul Play since it opened in 1979. Black walls, black shelving, and an unilluminated secret door are Foul Play's furnishings, housing used and new mystery, horror, spy, suspense, and true crime books. The blood-red neon welcomes you into this congested alcazar of murder and mayhem; the staff awaits you.

SERVICES • catalogs, will buy rare mysteries

Branch
1465 Second Ave (76-Upper East Side)
517-3222
M-Sat 12–10, Sun 11:30–6:30

Murder Ink

2486 Broadway 10025
(92-Upper West Side)
488-8123
M-Sun 10–7

Murder Ink is the world's first mystery bookstore, carrying new and used mystery and suspense fiction titles as well as true crime and suspense books, spy/thrillers, Edgar nominees and winners, and reference books on mystery writing. A good selection of mysteries for children and young adults is also available. A highlighted staff recommendations section rounds off this noteworthy store where many out-of-print titles and anything you'll want on Sherlock Holmes can be found.

SERVICES · catalog, shipping

Mysterious Bookshop

129 W 56 St 10019
(Sixth-Midtown West)
765-0900
M-Sat 11–7

The Mysterious Bookshop opened in April 1979 on Friday the 13th, and it provides an uncannily comprehensive collection of new, used, and rare (and weird) mystery, crime, suspense, detective fiction, and espionage books. The shop has two floors: the ground floor houses Mysterious's huge paperback selection, and upstairs are new and used hardcovers, including fiction and true crime titles, first editions, reference, and writing. The editorial offices of the Mysterious Press and the *Armchair Detective* magazine (published by Mysterious owner, Otto Penzler) are in the building as well. Mysteriobibliophiles can join the shop's Crime Collectors Club, which makes autographed and even inscribed first editions regularly available.

SERVICES • catalogs, Crime Collectors Club, o/p searches, shipping

Also see SCIENCE FICTION—SCIENCE FICTION, MYSTERIES AND MORE!

Native American Studies

By appointment only:

Bob Fein Books
150 Fifth Ave Rm 841 10011
807-0489

antiquarian books on North and South American Indians, particularly art and history, some new titles; pre-Columbian art

Also see MUSEUM—NATIONAL MUSEUM OF THE AMERICAN INDIAN

Natural History

By appointment only:

Jutta Buck, Antiquarian Book and Print Sellers
4 E 95 St 10128
289-4577 (fax 797-1189)

antiquarian books on natural history, botany, and nature; illustrated books

Naturalist's Bookshelf
540 W 114 St 10025
865-6202 (fax 865-2718)

antiquarian and used collection of natural history, and related
art and biographies; catalog available

And:

The Nature Company
8 Fulton St 10038
422-8510
M-Sat 10–9, Sun 11–7

This nationwide store and
catalog company has a fine se-
lection of new natural history titles on the second level of their
gift store located at the South Street Seaport. The stock includes
adult and children's titles in such fields as nature, animal and
plant life, earth and environmental sciences, astronomy, art and
photographic essays.

See ANTIQUARIAN, MUSEUM—AMERICAN MUSEUM OF NATURAL HISTORY

Nautical

While there isn't a bookstore devoted strictly to nautical books,
there are two general seafaring shops with good book departments:

The Chandlery:
A Seaport Museum Shop

209 Water St 10038
669-9455
M-Sun 10–6

In a corner, tucked away from the nautical gear, accessories, model boats, and general gift items, is a small room filled with new books on sailing, ocean liners, nautical guides, references, photographic essays, boat building, maritime and naval history, the Titanic, and highlighted fiction by such sea lovers as Melville, O'Brian, Forester, and others.

And, New York Nautical at 140 West Broadway at Thomas Street is a nautical chart store that devotes a section of the shop to nautical books and guides as well as titles on navigation, maritime law, and sea wrecks. Their number is 962-4522, hours 9–5 Monday through Friday, 9–12 on Saturdays.

New Age

East West Books

78 Fifth Ave 10011
(13-Greenwich Village)
243-5994
M-Sat 10–7, Sun 12–6

An "oasis of tranquility" is what East West provides in many forms. Their extensive collection of periodicals and new books covers Eastern and Western religions, and comparative studies, in addition to meditation, yoga, health, healing, psychology, astrology, cooking, metaphysics, and spirituality. Recordings of the New Age music, which play continuously, are for sale along with oils, incense, crystals, and jewelry.

East West Books is also the home of the Himalayan Institute of New York, where the process of personal growth and transformation continues. Yoga, meditation, cooking, health, nutrition, and relaxation classes are available at this center, while bus trips away from the congested city and into the calmer countryside are provided. Whatever the direction of your path, your pilgrim's mind, body, and spirit will be welcomed here.

MAIN SECTIONS • American Indian/astrology/bodyworks/Buddhism/ Chinese philosophy/Christianity/consciousness/family life/health/Himalayan Institute/Indian philosophy/Jung/meditation and yoga/metaphysics/natural medicine/nutrition/psychology/Sufism/Western mysticism/women's studies

OTHER HIGHLIGHTED SECTIONS • ancients/birth/comparative religions/homeopathy/Judaica/martial arts/recovery/science/Zen

Branches
568 Columbus Ave (86-Upper West Side)
787-7552
M-F 11–7, Sat & Sun 12–6

67 Cooper Sq 10003 (Third-East Village)
475-4459
M-Sun 11–7

Esoterica Bookstore
61 Fourth Ave 10003 (9-East Village)
529-9808
M-Th 11–10, F & Sat 11–11, Sun 12–5

Every conceivable subject within the category of New Age is represented on the shelves of Esoterica. More than half of the books are new, many are used, and there is a display case filled with rare and out-of-print esoteric volumes. The store is very serene and bright, even the shelves are lightly stained, and

Indian music is constantly playing. One of the helpful staff members will gladly show you any deck from what may be the city's largest selection of tarot cards.

MAIN SECTIONS • AIDS/astrology/Celtic and Norse/Christianity/ course in miracles/creativity/fiction/food—cooking, herbs, nutrition/goddesses/health/Hindu scriptures/Hinduism and India/Islam/Judaism/Native American/New Age/Nichiren Soshu/out-of-prints/past lives and channeling/psychology/science—conservation, nature, new/spiritual teachers/Tibetan Buddhism/Zen

OTHER HIGHLIGHTED SECTIONS • ancient civilizations/anthropology/architecture/bodywork/children's/comparative religions/crystals/ dance/discordia/drama/dreams/Egypt/gay studies/Gandhi/Gurdjieff/handwriting analysis/I Ching/Kabbalah/lycanthropy/magic/martial arts/music/ numbers/palmistry/parenting/philosophy/prophecy/prosperity/psychic/ recovery/runes/sexuality/Steiner/Taoism/tarot/theology/travel/UFOs/ vampirology/women's studies/yoga and meditation/Yogananda

SERVICES • library purchases, shipping, special orders

Quest Bookshop of the New York Theosophical Society

240 E 53 St 10022 (Second-Midtown East)
758-5521
M-W & F 10–6, Th 10–8, Sat 12–5

Harmony among people and the comparative studies of religion, philosophy, and science are the objectives of the worldwide Theosophical Society. Only by realizing what the Indian mystic and poet Kabir called "the One in all things" can these objectives be achieved. The bookstore at this center, where classes, lectures, and workshops are given, carries an in-depth selection of new hardcover and paperback titles to facilitate each individual's search for truth. This quest officially began in 1875 when Helena Blavatsky and Henry Olcott founded the New York Theosophical Society.

MAIN SECTIONS · American Indian/art and music/astrology/author sections/Bhagavad Gita/Chinese/comparative religions/consciousness/culture and communities/death and reincarnation/health and healing/I Ching/literature and poetry/mantras/meditation/men's studies/mind science/mysticism/myth and symbols/nature and ecology/numerology/nutrition/philosophy/prophecy/psychism/psychology/recovery/religions—Buddhism, Christianity, Hinduism, Islam and Sufism, Judaism and Kabbalah/science/spiritual life/tarot/theosophy/women's studies/yoga

   Authors stocked in depth include, but are not limited to, the following: Bailey, Besant, Blavatsky, Brunton, Casteneda, Fox, Goldsmith, Hay, Hodson, Judge, Krishnamurti, Leadbeater, Mahatma, Olcott, Roberts, Steiner, and Swami Rama.

   Quest Books/The Theosophical Publishing House, founded over twenty-five years ago, is today a major publisher of a variety of theosophical books. All of the publications are available at the bookstore.

OTHER HIGHLIGHTED SECTIONS · alchemy/dreams/freemasonry/occult and magic/palmistry and handwriting/Rosecrucianism/Spanish books

SERVICES · catalog, shipping, special orders, student discounts

Samuel Weiser, Inc.
132 E 24 St 10010 (Lexington-Gramercy)
777-6363
M-W 9–6, Th & F 10–7, Sat 9:30–5:30, Sun 12–5

It seems Samuel Weiser's has been around long before the term *New Age* existed. The store opened in 1926, and remains an esteemed seller and publisher of mystical, spiritual, and magical books. The spacious and tranquil shop is the home of thousands of predominantly new paperbacks and used and out-of-print hardcovers. A display case holds a selection of rare titles, some dating as far back as the seventeenth century. Domestic and foreign periodicals are available, in addition to incense, tarot cards, and astrological charts. As you step down and into Weiser's you will encounter at the front desk one of the kindest clerks in what is described as "the world's largest metaphysical bookstore."

MAIN SECTIONS • art/astrology/bodywork/Buddhism/consciousness/ M. P. Hall/holistic health/hypnosis/I Ching/India/inspiration/literature/ magic/mental/metaphysics/mythology and psyche/occult/philosophy/psychic/psychology/self-help/R. Steiner/tarot and Kabbalah

OTHER HIGHLIGHTED SECTIONS • African religions/children's/ earth religions/herbs/Islam/martial arts/Native American/numerology/ prophecy/theosophy/Tibet/women/Zen

SERVICES • catalog, library purchases, shipping, special services

New York

Citybooks

61 Chambers St 10007 (Broadway-Financial)
669-8245
M-F 9–5

Citybooks is a government agency providing many publications geared to making life a bit easier for New Yorkers. Pamphlets and books on building and housing laws, fire codes, historic reports, budgets, housing studies, landmark development, tenant rights, and even a bit of history are for sale along with some memorabilia. Omnis civitas corpus est.

SERVICES • shipping

New York Bound Bookshop

50 Rockefeller Plaza 10020
(49-Midtown West)
245-8503
M-F 10–6, Sat 12–4

A few years ago an archeological excavation began in lower Manhattan to unearth the foundations of old structures in an attempt to further understand the early days of our city's history. Whether

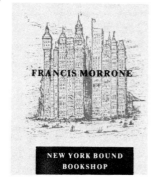

FRANCIS MORRONE

NEW YORK BOUND
BOOKSHOP

dusty digs tempt you or not, a bit of armchair archeology and history may. If so, you are definitely New York Bound. This store is wonderful. It carries virtually every book in print that takes New York as a subject, and it also stocks a wide and exhaustive selection of used and out-of-print titles. Barbara Cohen and her partner, Judith Stonehill, are as resourceful and helpful as the volumes, prints, antique postcards and photographs they acquire and sell. They encourage browsing and even provide the armchair.

MAIN SECTIONS · architecture and city planning/boroughs/business history/children's/crime/fiction/guidebooks/history/immigrant experience/journalism/Manhattan/politics/Edith Wharton
     Several books on the cuisine of New York City and the metropolis's nightlife are also for sale.

SERVICES · catalog, shipping, special orders

Open by appointment only:

Judith and Peter Klemperer
400 Second Ave 10010
684-5970

antiquarian books on New York City and state, related nineteenth-century fiction

See also MUSEUM—NEW-YORK HISTORICAL SOCIETY MUSEUM SHOP, MUSEUM OF THE CITY OF NEW YORK

Occult

Magickal Childe, Inc.
35 W 19 St 10011 (Fifth-Chelsea)
242-7182
M-Sat 11–8, Sun 12–6

Books on the occult, in addition to ritualistic supplies, such as swords, daggers, talismans, and candles, are for sale in this long dark store staffed by a cast of characters one might describe as idiosyncratic (but not, of course, by this writer). In the center of the shop, surrounded by books, are more books and a mind-boggling supply of herbs and powders. The books are relatively new, mostly in paperback, and a bit dusty. What's hidden inside them remains to be seen.

MAIN SECTIONS • anthropology/astrology/Cayce/Christianity/Crowley/ dreams/Egyptian/ESP/feminism/hermetics/herbalism/history of magic/ Huna/magick/mythology/Native American/numerology/palmistry/satanism/self-help/Seth/tarot/theosophy/UFOs/Wicca

SERVICES • catalog, shipping, special orders
If you want to have your cards read, there is always a reader on the premises.

Photography

A Photographer's Place
133 Mercer St 10012 (Prince-Soho)
431-9358
M-F 10-30–6:30, Sat 11–5

Thousands of titles fill the shelves in the city's sole general photography bookstore.
Vintage photographs and cameras are displayed on the brick walls painted white with black trim. New, used, remaindered, and out-of-print titles make up the stock, which includes excellent selections of biographies, monographs, photographic theory, and technical volumes. The section on photojournalism is extensive, as is the display of magazines and journals.

MAIN SECTIONS • camera manuals/collecting/collections/history/monographs/out-of-prints/photo essays/photo journalism/photography series/sale books/technical—compositions, by genre, processing/theory/topographic

SERVICES • appraisals, catalog, library purchases, shipping

The following booksellers are open by appointment only:

Howard Daitz—Photographica
328 W 20 St 10011
929-8987

nineteenth- and twentieth-century images and books

VF Germack Professional Photography Collectors
1199 Park Ave 10028
289-8411

antiquarian and out-of-print photography books

Janet Lehr, Inc.
P.O. Box 617 10028
288-1802

antiquarian and used photography books, Americana and Asian concentration

Andrew Makowsky Fine Books
63 Downing St 7B 10014
675-7789

used and antiquarian photography books and images

Fred and Elizabeth Pajerski
225 W 25 St 4K 10001
255-6501

antiquarian photography books, catalog available

Vasta Images
95 Van Dam St 10013
243-347

antiquarian photography and surrealism books

Also:

International Center of Photography
1130 Fifth Ave 10128 (94-Upper East Side)
860-1751
T 11–8, W-Sun 11–6

and

International Center of Photography Midtown
1133 Sixth Ave 10036 (43-Midtown West)
768-4680
T 11–8, W-Sun 11–6

Both centers have small but well-stocked shops with monographs, theory, history, and technical new books as well as a
selection of periodicals. Books related to current exhibitions are
for sale, as are past and present exhibition catalogs. In addition
to the shows the centers offer workshops, lectures, classes, and
provide photo labs. The uptown ICP is located in a picture-
postcard perfect Georgian townhouse.

SERVICES · shipping

Witkin Gallery
415 W Broadway 4th fl 10012 (Prince-Soho)
925-5510
T-F 11–6, Sat 12–6

Vintage and contemporary photographic works are on display,
and related books, both in and out-of-print, are for sale.

SERVICES · shipping

Check ART listings for shops with photography sections. Many specialty booksellers sell
photographic volumes related to their particular subject.

Poetry

It is difficult
to get the news from poems
yet men die miserably every day
for lack
of what is found there.
William Carlos Williams,
"Asphodel, That Greeny Flower"

Unfortunately, this city lacks a bookstore of poetry, but try THE GOTHAM BOOK MART (see p. 25). Displayed in their poetry alcove is a fraction of what is hidden in their basement.

Political Science

Revolution Books
13 E 16 St 10003
(Union Sq W-Chelsea)
691-3345
M-Sat 10–7, Sun 12–5

This bookstore, staffed primarily by volunteers, is New York's "political and promotional center" of the Revolutionary Communist Party. The stock consists of new titles written from Marxist and socialist perspectives in philosophy, literature, and the sciences, including historical accounts of the subjugation and struggles of working-class and oppressed peoples worldwide. Used and out-of-print books are shelved in the back of the store, next to an extensive selection of periodicals in many languages. In addition to Revolution's stock of English,

French, and Spanish books, they also carry Marxist texts in Chinese, Farsi, and Turkish. Discussions of the Revolutionary Worker Newspaper are held weekly, in addition to regular meetings on related topics.

MAIN SECTIONS • Africa/Arab east/arts/Caribbean/Central America/ Cuba/historical experience of proletarian revolution/Lenin/literature—African American, American, Asian-American, Caribbean, Latino, Native American/Mao/Marx and Engels/media/occupied Palestine and Israel/philosophy and cultural studies/Revolutionary Communist Party/Revolutionary International Party/South Africa/struggle of black people in the U.S./ U.S. imperialism/women's oppression and women's liberation

OTHER HIGHLIGHTED SECTIONS • anthropology/atheism/children's/Eastern Europe/ecology and environment/Germany/health and psychology/Native American studies/religion/science/Stalin/U.S. history

BOOKS IN FRENCH • Engels/la literature/Lenin/l'oppression des femmes/Mao/Marx/la philosophie

BOOKS IN SPANISH • America Latina/economía política/educación/ Engels/filosofía/ideología/la República Dominicana/la revolución rusa/Lenin/literatura/Mao/Marx/mujeres/Nicaragua/religion

SERVICES • discussion groups, newsletters, shipping, special orders

Unity Book Center
237 W 23 St 10011 (Eighth-Chelsea)
242-2934
M-F 10:30–6, Sat 11–4

In the building housing Unity is the Workers School for Marxist-Leninist Studies, both affiliated with the site's main tenant—the Office of the Central Committee of the Communist Party USA. The shop specializes in the writings of Marx, Lenin, and Engels, in addition to other communist authors and writers of oppression. Imports from Spain and Mexico fill the Spanish book sections, and there are a good number of children's books imported from Russia and translated into English. You can pick up for free a copy of the U.S. Communist Party's Constitution, join the Young Communists' League, and attend one of the many classes, workshops, and cultural forums held regularly at the center.

MAIN SECTIONS · children's/Engels/history—U.S./international affairs/labor/Lenin/libros en español/literature and poetry/Marx/political economy/Soviet literature

OTHER HIGHLIGHTED SECTIONS · black studies/cookbooks and health/dictionaries/Dover/philosophy

SERVICES · newsletters, shipping

Professional

McGraw-Hill Bookstore

1221 Sixth Ave 10020 (48-Midtown West)
512-4100
M-Sat 10–5:45

This large bookstore specializing in books for professionals in several fields is located in the basement of the McGraw-Hill building. From the cashier's cyclical desk at the shop's entrance shelves radiate outwards. Although at first the design appears awkward, professionally speaking, it works. The business, management, computer, and engineering sections are stocked with new hardcovers, quality paperbacks, reference, and textbooks. In addition to the huge selections in these professions are books in the well-represented sciences. And, finally, to please the professional who likes to leave her job at the workplace, books in the arts and humanities are also offered.

MAIN SECTIONS · accounting/advertising/audio and video/aviation/ banking/biology/careers/chemical engineering/civil engineering/current affairs/economics/electrical engineering/electronic engineering/environmental science/graphic arts/health/industrial engineering/investments and finance/management—general, personnel, sales/marketing/mathematics/ mechanical engineering/medicine/mergers and acquisitions/options and futures/physics/popular sciences/psychology/reference—atlases, college guides, dictionaries, exam guides, foreign language, technical dictionaries/ small business/strategic planning/taxation/travel guides—domestic and foreign

OTHER HIGHLIGHTED SECTIONS • architecture/astronomy/automotive and railroad/biography/business communication/children's/cooking/ earth science/education/ESL/gardening and nature/general interest/history/home maintenance/hydrology and waste management/interior design/ law/literature/media/mystery and suspense/New York/office training/personal business/real estate/religion and philosophy/romance/sale books/science fiction/sports/tourism/wine industry/writing and grammar

The computer section is divided into the following categories: artificial intelligence/Autocad/business/business applications/communications/computer architecture/computer languages—C, Cobol, Pascal/Database/desktop publishing/dictionaries and directories/general/graphics/Intel books/Macintosh/microprocessors/pocket guides/software engineering/systems/Unix/windows/word processing/X-Windows

SERVICES • shipping, special orders
A McGraw Hill Publications catalog is available at the store.

NYU Professional Bookstore

530 LaGuardia Pl 10012 (Bleecker-Greenwich Village)
998-4680
M-Th 10–7, F 10–6, Sat 12–6

What used to be the New York University Law Book Store has now become the school's professional bookstore. However, the store still dedicates half its space to law books, and the other half now displays primarily business books. The technical and scholarly texts serve students and professionals, although bestselling popular titles are also for sale. Faculty publications are highlighted.

MAIN SECTIONS—BUSINESS • accounting/economics/finance/financial markets and investments/information systems/management/marketing/ marketing concepts and strategies/operations management/quantitative methods/strategy and policy

OTHER HIGHLIGHTED SECTIONS—BUSINESS • career guides/ economics—micro and macro/global finance/international business/managing organizational behavior/statistics and operations research/taxation
Harvard Business Review and Arco series are also stocked.

MAIN SECTIONS—LAW • administrative and constitutional law/clinical advocacy/corporate and commercial law/criminal justice/international legal studies/jurisprudence/personal and family law/practice and procedure/property law/public services

OTHER HIGHLIGHTED SECTIONS—LAW · contracts/criminal/
paralegal/procedure/torts

Law hornbooks, LL.M. Income Taxation guides, and the following series are also available: Black Letter, Casebook, Emanuel, Gilbert and Nutshell.

SERVICES · shipping, special orders

Psychology

Book Store of the New York
Psychoanalytic Institute

247 E 82 St 10028 (Second-Upper East Side)
772-8282
MWTh 2:30–8:30

This is a very small bookstore—actually part of the institution's library—which sells a limited selection of both new and used books on Freud, and on the history and clinical practice of psychoanalysis.

SERVICES · catalog, shipping

Brunner-Mazel, Inc.

19 Union Sq W 10003 (17-Chelsea)
924-3344
M-F 9–4:45 (Th til 6:30), Sat 10:30–3:30 (Sept-May)

Brunner-Mazel carries the finest selection in the city of new books in psychiatry, psychoanalysis, and psychotherapy for the specialist, therapist, doctor, or interested lay person. The paperback and hardcover scholarly and professional titles are arranged by author's last name in one huge collection that includes the company's own publications. Magination Press and Karnac Books are highlighted separately, as are books on and by Freud and Winnicott. An excellent selection of reference works and journals are available, and only the very best trade titles are stocked. Tables and chairs are provided, and should you desire complete comfort, you can also purchase a pair of Freudian slippers.

SERVICES • catalog, shipping, special orders

Jung Foundation Book Service
29 E 39 St 10016 (Park-Midtown East)
697-6433 (fax 953-3989)
M-Th 10–7, F 11–3

Carl Jung believed that a person's primary task was to achieve harmony between the conscious and unconscious, and the Jung Foundation is dedicated to promoting this principle for both the individual and society. Classes, workshops, and lectures are held at this educational center, where the public is free to peruse the library's volumes (you must be a member to check out a title). New books for sale in the small store located within the townhouse include both paperback and hardcover editions of Jung's own works and Jungian studies, in addition to publications on dreams, mythology, and folktales.

SERVICES • catalog, shipping

Railroads

By appointment only:

Arnold Joseph
1140 Broadway Rm 701 10001
532-0019

over five thousand antiquarian, used, and new books on railroads (some on general transportation) and railroad ephemera

For additional books on railway travel, both past and present-day, see TRAVEL

Reference

Reference Book Center
175 Fifth Ave 10010 (23-Gramercy)
677-2160
M-F 10–4

If you wanted to know where the expression *twenty-three skiddoo* came from (or any other once fashionably mysterious saying), perhaps one of the numerous reference works at the Reference Book Center, located on the seventh floor of the Flatiron Building, might enlighten you. The two-room store has new and used dictionaries, encyclopedias, atlases, thesauri, almanacs, concordances, and some miscellaneous out-of-print editions.

MAIN SECTIONS · animals/art/black studies/business and law/classical world/dictionaries/foreign language dictionaries/geography and atlases/history and politics/literature and poetry/mathematics/medical/mythology, folklore, and occult/Native American/natural sciences and nature/performing arts/quotations/religion/science and discovery/social sciences/women's studies/young adult references

SERVICES · catalog, shipping, special orders

Also see FOREIGN LANGUAGE—LIBRAIRIE DE FRANCE for a complete line of technical dictionaries in foreign languages and LEXICOGRAPHY for antiquarian reference works.

Remainders and Discounted Books

Chapter and Verse
12 St. Mark's Pl 10003 (Second-East Village)
M-Th 11–11, F 11–12, Sun 12–10

Chapter and Verse is a brand-new, long, and narrow two-room store in the heart of the East Village (so new, in fact, that at the time of this writing the phone had not yet been installed). The front room is dedicated completely to periodicals, magazines, and journals of various subjects and the back room, with a small mezzanine, houses discounted books and remainders.

Books are reduced in price at least 10 percent—most of them are at half their retail value. The general remainder section carries changing popular titles in the arts and humanities.

MAIN SECTIONS • biography/children's/fiction/history/remainders/travel

OTHER HIGHLIGHTED SECTIONS • art/criticism/film/health/music/mystery/philosophy/political economy/reference/science and nature/science fiction/women's studies

Drougas Books

34 Carmine Street 10014 (Bleecker-Greenwich Village)
229-0078
M-W & F 12–9, Sat & Sun 2–9

This small bookstore is filled with "un-oppressive and non-imperialist" bargain books, remainders, and wonderful imports. The main sections remain constant, but the stock within them varies. Miscellaneous titles cover the display tables, and these, too, change often. This bookstore merits regular visits, and a buy-it-when-you-see-it attitude, because the many good discounted titles disappear quickly.

MAIN SECTIONS • Africa and African writers/art/drama/Eastern philosophy/Latin American studies and writers/literature/music/photography/reference/women's studies

OTHER HIGHLIGHTED SECTIONS • animals/biography/William Blake/humor/Jungian studies/mythology/Native American/New York/poetry/psychology/travel

Paperback Discounter

2517 Broadway 10025 (93-Upper West Side)
662-1718
M-Sun 11–11

This half-book, half-video store is filled with an eclectic mix of half-price, discounted, and primarily used mass-market paperbacks. New best-sellers are for sale. Fiction, science fiction, mystery, and romance are the subjects well covered. The win-

dow book display shares space with VCR repair ads and video signs—the owner has a deal where you can get video rental credit for your old paperbacks if you're a store member. In addition, he will special order almost any new title.

SERVICES · special orders

Ruby's Book Sale
119 Chambers St 10007 (Church-Tribeca)
732-8676
M-F 10–6, Sat 10–5:30

Although Ruby's isn't as large as it once was, it is still a good-size store that carries thousands of discounted new releases, hardcover popular remainders, and half-price used paperbacks. Displayed on tables and shelves in the front of the shop are the remainders, and the huge paperback selection is in the rear. On one side of the store is Ruby's incredible collection of discounted back-issue magazines and journals, each one wrapped in its own plastic cover for protection.

MAIN SECTIONS • Hardcover:
art/children's/cooking/gift books/health/history/literature/military/music/photography/religion/sports/travel
    Paperbacks:
biography/computers/fiction and literature/history—American, world/mystery/romance

OTHER HIGHLIGHTED SECTIONS • Hardcover:
Americana/animals/antiques/architecture/black interest/collectibles/crafts/gardening/home repairs/nature/reference
    Paperbacks:
astrology/cooking/health/humor/philosophy/psychology/religion/science/Shakespeare/sociology/sports/women's studies/young adult books

Science and Medicine

Book Scientific
18 E 16 St 2nd fl 10011 (Union Sq W-Chelsea)
206-1310 (fax 675-4230)
M-Sat 10–5

Scientific and technical books related to chemistry, engineering, mathematics, physics, and reference works are stocked at Book Scientific. Most of the volumes are new, although there is a fine selection of used texts at a discount. The titles are very technical; the store does not carry popular works. Students and university faculty receive a discount with identification.

SERVICES • shipping, special orders

General Medical Book Company
310 E 26 St 10010 (First-Gramercy)
532-0756 (fax 889-5756)
M-F 10–6, Sat 10:30–5

The General Medical Book Company has been serving health professionals, doctors, nurses, dentists, and students since

1918. The store is filled with every imaginable technical medical book. No popular titles are stocked. The owner provides a complete listing of texts in the store, and makes every attempt to facilitate overnight delivery, if that's what the doctor orders.

MAIN SECTIONS · AIDS/allergy/anatomy/anesthesiology/biochemistry/ cardiology/critical care/dentistry/dermatology/diagnosis/dictionaries/emergency medicine/endocrinology/family practice/gastroenterology/genetics/ geriatrics/hematology/infectious disease/internal medicine/tropical medicine/laboratory medicine/microbiology/neonatology/neurology/nursing/nutrition/obstetrics and gynecology/oncology/ophthalmology/orthopedics/otolaryngology/pathology/pediatrics/pharmacology/physiology/public health/ psychiatry/radiology/respiratory system/rheumatology/sports medicine/surgery/plastic and reconstructive surgery/toxicology/urology/veterinary

The various series titles for sale here include:
Appleton and Lange Review/Board Review/House Officer/Lange Clinical Manuals, Handbooks/Little Brown Spirals and Handbooks/Medical Board Review/Medical Examination Review/Medical Intelligence Unit/National Medical/Oklahoma Notes/Pretest/Thieme Flexibooks/Yearbook Handbooks

SERVICES · catalog, shipping, special orders

Martayan Lan
48 E 57 St 10022 (Fifth-Midtown East)
308-0018 (fax 308-0074)
M-F 9:30–5:30

Several hundred antiquarian and illustrated books from the fifteenth to eighteenth centuries on the histories of science and medicine are on display at Martayan Lan. Antique globes round out the stock, which also includes rare atlases, natural history, and technology titles.

SERVICES · appraisals, catalog, o/p searches, shipping

Mount Sinai Hospital Medical Bookstore
Madison Ave @ 99 St Box 1025 10029
241-2665
M-F 9–5

This is a small bookstore located inside the hospital and stocked with new medical texts and reference works for professionals and staff members. Subjects covered include anatomy, medicine, neurology, obstetrics, pediatrics, psychology, and surgery. Dictionaries, exam reviews, and study guides are available, in addition to a small selection of best-selling general trade books and paperback computer books.

NYU Medical Book Center
550 First Ave 10016
(32-Gramercy)
263-5444
M-F 10–5

In one of the many buildings in New York University's Medical School and Center is a small bookstore carrying medical textbooks for NYU students and professional staff. Medical references and study guides are also for sale as well as the usual college store stock of stationery and school supplies.

MAIN SECTIONS • anatomy/anesthesiology/biochemistry/cardiology/dermatology/emergency medicine/endocrinology/gastrointestinal/genetics/hematology/infectious medicine/microbiology/neurology/nutrition/obstetrics and gynecology/oncology/ophthalmology/orthopedics/otolaryology/pathology/pediatrics/physiology/pulmonary and respiratory/pharmacology/psychiatry/radiology/surgery/urology

The store also stocks medical handbooks, manuals and references, in addition to the following series: Appleton and Lange, Lange, McGraw-Hill, and Williams and Williams.

By appointment only:

Jonathan A. Hill, Bookseller
470 West End Ave 10023
496-7856 (fax 496-9182)

antiquarian books on science and medicine; early printed books

Bruce Ramer, Experimenta Old and Rare Books

401 E 80 St 24 10021
772-6211 (fax 650-9032)

antiquarian titles on science and medicine, in addition to technology and natural history; sixteenth and seventeenth century rare books

Also see GENERAL—BARNES AND NOBLE, TRAVEL—RICHARD B. ARKWAY. And, for rare and out-of-print medical books, see USED—ARGOSY.

Science Fiction and Fantasy

Forbidden Planet

821 Broadway 10003 (12-East Village)
473-1576
M & T 10–7, W-F 10–7:30, Sat 10–7, Sun 12–7

Forbidden Planet is, as it claims to be, *the* Science Fiction Megastore. On one-half of the megaground floor is its extensive selection of fantasy, horror, and science fiction paperbacks, along with hardcover new releases plus showcased Hugo and Nebula Award winners. American and Japanese new and vintage comics and magazines take up the remaining floor space. In the basement are more comics, robot toys, ghastly games, and the most astonishing collection of weird masks, which take up a good-size wall. The books downstairs are series titles: Battletech, Choose Your Own Adventure, Dr. Who, and Forgotten Realms. A variety of alien visitors drop in regularly. Just recently, Robo Cop appeared. If any planet is forbidden in here, it's probably Earth. Everything and everybody else is from another planet.

Branch:
227 E 59 St (Third-Midtown East)
751-4386
M-Sat 11:30–8:30, Sun 12–7

SERVICES • catalog, shipping, special orders

Science Fiction Shop
168 Thompson St 10014 (Houston-Greenwich Village)
473-3010
M 11–7, T & W 11–8, Th-Sat 11–9, Sun 12–6

As you step down into the Science Fiction Shop you'll see a sign that reads, "If it is not on the shelves, it is probably out of print." This just might be true. On the shelves is an extensive selection of paperback science fiction—arranged alphabetically by author's last name—including novels, anthologies, and books in series. Many of these are imported and some are used or out-of-print. Fantasy and horror titles are also stocked, in addition to magazines, theoretical and reference works.

SERVICES • catalog, shipping, special orders

Science Fiction, Mysteries and More!

140 Chambers St 10007 (West Broadway-Financial)
385-8798
M-F 11:30–7, Sat & Sun 2:30–6:30

Advertising itself as New York's "only combination mystery, science fiction, espionage and fantasy bookstore," SFMM! carries used and new books, plus comics, magazines, and audio tapes. Many out-of-print books are also for sale; a comic subscription service is offered; writing workshops are held in the store; and the "expert staff" seems to find a reason to throw a party at least once a month. Finally, Rocket and Dagger Readings by various sci-fi and fantasy writers happen on various Wednesday nights.

SERVICES · author signings and readings, library purchases, o/p searches, shipping

Scientology—See ADDITIONAL LISTINGS

Self-help

Choices: The Recovery Bookshop

220 E 78 St 10021 (Second-Upper East Side)
794-3858
T-F 11–7, Sat 11–6, Sun 12–4 (closed Sundays in July and August)

This full-service, well-stocked bookstore carries a complete line of new titles related to the various addictions plaguing contemporary society. Popular self-help authors are well-represented; however, professional books are also on the shelves. Oft-repeated sayings and words of wisdom are printed on displayed mugs, tee shirts, and note cards. The shop carries the complete line of Hazelden publications, and has exhaustive selections of books on drug abuse, alcoholism, and the 12-step program. The friendly staff members are as helpful as the books.

MAIN SECTIONS • abuse—emotional, sexual/alcoholism/children's/ death/drugs/family/Hazelden publications/HIV/meditation books/profes- sional texts/relationships/12 step

Also:

Stress Less Step

48 E 61 St 10021
826-6222
M-F 10–9, Sat 10–6

This center for "ongoing stress control and physical well-being" has a small selection of books for sale in the waiting room on such subjects as yoga, PMS, stress, relaxation, and massage. Massages, body wraps, facials, and additional stress-less joys are available.

Sports

Sportswords, Ltd.

1475 Third Ave
(83rd-Upper East Side)
772-8729 (fax 772-8809)
M-F 11–8, Sat 10:30–7,
Sun 11–5:45

This brand-new, brightly lit, and comfortable shop sells new paperbacks and hardcovers on every sport—including game strategy, biographies, history, and trivia books. A wide selec- tion of reference books are also for sale, as are oversize photog- raphy volumes. Young readers interested in sports will be able to choose among the many fiction and nonfiction titles on the shelves. Duas tantem res anxius optat, Panem et Circenses. If you can't attend, at least you can read about them.

MAIN SECTIONS • For each of the following sports Sportswords stocks biographies, histories, references, and books on game strategy: baseball/basketball/bicyling/bowling/fishing/football/golf/hockey/lacrosse/ martial arts/riding/running/sailing/skiing/tennis

OTHER HIGHLIGHTED SECTIONS · card price guides/children's and young adults—fiction and non/fitness and training/reference/travel guides/ trivia books

SERVICES · shipping, special orders

By appointment only:

Larry Lawrence Rare Sports
150 Fifth Ave Rm 842 10011 (20-Chelsea)
362-8593

rare and out-of-print books on most all sports, ranging from books on boxing published in the eighteenth century to out-of-print baseball biographies; frequently issued catalog listings available

Sufism

Sufi Books
225 West Broadway 10013
(White-Tribeca)
334-5212 (fax 334–5214)
M-F 11–7, Sat 11–6:30

This strikingly austere, almost reverential shop is plain and yet elegant in its decor. It is a narrow, rectangular space with three walls of dark-stained wood shelving; a wooden table with a glass display for illustrated volumes runs down its center. New books are neatly arranged, and the serious mood is enhanced by a recording in the background of the call to prayer. The sections on Sufism, contemporary Sufism, and Sufi saints are extensively stocked.

MAIN SECTIONS · contemporary Sufism/Hadith/healing/Islam/Koran/ mysticism/Sheikh Muzaffer/Sufi saints/Sufism

OTHER HIGHLIGHTED SECTIONS · Buddhism/children's/Christianity/Hinduism/Judaism

SERVICES · catalog, shipping, special orders

Theosophy—see NEW AGE

Travel

Richard B. Arkway, Inc.
538 Madison Ave 10022 (54-Midtown East)
751-8135 (fax 832-5389)
M-F 9–5

Antiquarian volumes on travel and early voyages are among the rare books for sale here, with a particularly noteworthy section on the Far East. Antique maps, charts, and atlases are displayed throughout the shop. Mr. Arkway's second interest is medicine and early science, of which he maintains an equally representative collection.

SERVICES • appraisals, catalog

British Travel Bookshop
40 W 57 St 3rd fl 10019 (Fifth-Midtown West)
765-0898
M-F 9–5

If you want to be in England regardless of whether it's April or not, this official British tourist agency carries a good selection of travel guides. Many of the titles are imported, but they also stock a variety of popular travel publications from the U.S. In addition to maps the office sells hotel, sightseeing, restaurant, and road guides and offers a variety of travel services.

SERVICES • shipping

Complete Traveller Bookstore
199 Madison Ave 10016
(35-Midtown East)
685-9007 (fax 982-7628)
M-F 9–7, Sat 10–6, Sun 12–5

If you are an armchair voyager, or about-to-depart trekker or tourist, all your

printed traveling needs will be fulfilled at the Complete Traveller Bookstore. Two rooms are devoted to every imaginable site
around the world. The entrance room stocks new travel guides
for every state in the U.S. and, seemingly, every country on
every continent, with titles on particular cities, where to sleep,
where to roam, where to eat, and what to do. The second room,
the shop's newest addition, houses its collection of antiquarian
and rare travel guides and books. Back issues of WPA, Baede-
ker, and Cooke's guides are for sale, plus hundreds of recorded
tales of journeys made long ago. New and antiquarian maps are
included in this consummate collection.

SERVICES · shipping, special orders

Rand McNally—The Map and Travel Store
150 E 52 St 10022 (Lexington-Midtown East)
758-7488
M-F 9–6 (Th till 7), Sat 11–5

Rand McNally's store has been selling travel books and geographic paraphernalia in Manhattan for over forty years.
Atlases, globes, maps, and geographic games abound at the
front, while new books take up the back half of the shop.
Guides are separated into seven worldwide regions, plus a
section on New York. Pictorial regional cookbooks and foreign
language dictionaries are also for sale.

The Traveller's Bookstore
22 W 52 St 10019 (Fifth-Midtown West)
664-0995
M-F 9–6, Sat & Sun 11–5

The Traveller's Bookstore may not stock every title on your
destination, but you will find here one of the most interesting
collections of new books to choose from, and a knowledgeable,
well-traveled staff to guide you in making a purchase. Owners
Candace Olmsted and Jane Grossman read and even use, as

often as possible, the publications they sell, which include imports from Europe, Australia, New Zealand, and South America. The store is divided into regions with guidebooks, travelogues, nonfiction musings, and picture books in each division. Even a few novels and mysteries are stocked, provided, of course, that they offer insightful observations on their settings. The U.S. section includes guides to bed and breakfasts, country inns, antiques shopping, and discourses on regional foods. Maps and travel accessories are also for sale among the books you'll not likely find in another store. This is a highly recommended point of departure.

SERVICES • catalog, shipping, special orders

Also:

Civilized Traveller
1072 Third Ave 10021 (63-Upper East Side)
758-8305
M-Sat 10–7, Sun 12–5

This upscale travel store has a modest collection of domestic and foreign guidebooks and maps among the accessories, conveniences, gadgets, and suitcases designed to ease the traveler's load. Store branches are located at 2003 Broadway at 68th St and 2 World Trade Center; both keep the hours noted above.

Downeast Enterprises
73 Spring St 10012 (Broadway-Soho)
925-2632
M-Sat 11–6

Nietzsche said, "A few hours of mountain climbing turn a rascal and a saint into two pretty similar creatures. Fatigue is the shortest way to Equality and Fraternity—and, in the end, Liberty will surrender to Sleep." To facilitate this enterprise Downeast makes backpacks, repairs tents and hiking gear, and sells a fine selection of mountain climbing and hiking guides.

SERVICES • shipping

For antiquarian books on railway travel see RAILROADS—ARNOLD JOSEPH. For Women's Interests see EROTICA—EVE'S GARDEN; GAY AND LESBIAN—JUDITH'S ROOM (also A DIFFERENT LIGHT and OSCAR WILDE BOOKSHOPS), LITERATURE—PAULETTE ROSE; for titles on health issues particular to women, see SELF-HELP and YOGA; for scholarly and academic titles in women's studies, see GENERAL—BARNARD BOOKFORUM.

Yoga

Integral Yoga Bookshop
227 W 13 St 10011 (Eighth-Greenwich Village)
929-0586
M-F 10–8:30, Sat 10–5:30

The bookshop at the Integral Yoga Institute carries a fine selection of new books (mostly paperbacks) on yoga, meditation, Buddhism, spiritual growth, and health care. Sri Swami Satchidananda says that each moment should be a celebration, which is "possible only if you keep your mind in good shape." You can begin to do this at IYI's bookstore, and, if you want to keep your body in equally good shape, you may drop in on one of their many yoga classes.

MAIN SECTIONS · affirmations/Buddha/family and parenting/meditation/physical health—Ayurveda, Chinese medicine, herbs, mind and body/ psychology and spiritual healing and growth/relationships and sexuality/Sri Swami Satchidananda/Sri Swami Sivananda/Taoism/women's health and concerns—addiction, body image, food/yoga and Hinduism/Zen Buddhism

SERVICES · shipping

One of the joys of writing a book such as this is the discovery of an oversight and, of course, the opening of a new shop. Here are some additional listings.

GENERAL

Abandoned Books Café

955 West End Ave 10025 (107-Morningside Heights)
864–8840
M-Sun 10–11

limited selections of new and used books in the humanities and social sciences

Verso Books

128 Eighth Ave 10011 (16-Chelsea)
620–3141
M-Th 10–10, F & Sat 10–midnight, Sun 11–10

full-scale new bookstore, some remainders, café to open soon

SPECIALTY

Art

George Feher Associates

15 W 39 St 10018 (Fifth-Midtown West)
840–5599
M-F 11–5

new titles on African, South American, and Asian art

Decorative Arts

By appointment only:

Dey Gosse
1150 Fifth Ave 10128
996–4629

antiquarian books on decorative and fine arts, Middle Eastern and South American art

Dental—see listings under SCIENCE AND MEDICINE and:

Kriser Dental Center Bookstore
342 E 26st 10010 (First-Gramercy)
998–9990
M-Th 11–7, F 11–5

extensive selection of new titles for the dental profession

Foreign Languages

Chinese

America East Book Co.
46 Bowery 10013 (Canal-Lower East Side)
233–4926
M-Sun 10–8

new titles on China and Chinese literature

Spanish

La Bohemia
3441 Broadway 10031 (140-Harlem)
862–5500
M-Sat 8–6

new Spanish books imported from Spain and Mexico, emphasis on literature

By appointment only:

Roig Spanish Books
29 W 19 St 10011
675–1047

new titles on Spanish language and literature

Judaica

By appointment only:

Isaac Mann
240 W 80 St 10025
666–1149

used hardcovers, Judaic studies, and the Holocaust

Photography

Aperture
20 E 23 St 10010 (Broadway-Gramercy)
505–5555
M-F 9–5

sells all Aperture Press publications in addition to a selection of new books by other publishers

Scientology

Dianetics Center
227 W 46 St 10036 (Broadway-Midtown West)
921–1210
M-F 9–10, Sat & Sun 9–7

new publications on scientology and books by L. Ron Hubbard

Christie's Book Department
502 Park Ave @ E 59 St 10022
546-1196
M-F 9:30–5:30

Christie's holds approximately four sales per year of antiquarian books and manuscripts. On the average each sale has 250 lots with a minimum value of five thousand dollars per lot. Write or call the book department for auction dates and/or to order a catalog, usually priced at thirty-five dollars.

Metropolitan Antiques Pavilion
110 W 19 St @ Sixth Ave 10011
463-0200
M-F 9–5

Approximately twelve times per year the Metropolitan Antiques Pavilion holds auctions of antiquarian books and modern first editions. Books are sold one at a time at an average price of one hundred dollars. Catalogues for each sale are available at a five-dollar cost. Call or write to request one, and if you want to be on their mailing list, they will send you announcements regularly of upcoming auctions.

Sotheby's Book Department
1334 York Ave @ E 72 St 10021
606-7000
M-F 9–5:30

Sales of antiquarian books and manuscripts are held four to six times per year, with at least two of the sales concentrating on Americana. Antiquarian auctions have six hundred lots on average; Americana auctions contain two hundred. Minimum value of each lot is two thousand dollars. Call the book department at the above number for information on the next sale. To subscribe to Sotheby's newsletter (twenty-five-dollar cost) or to receive a particular catalog (thirty-five-dollar cost) call 1-800-444-3709.

Swann Auction Gallery

104 E 25 St @ Park Ave 10010
254-4710
M-F 9:30–5:30

In business over fifty years, Swann is the first major American book auction house. They hold at least thirty-five sales per year of antiquarian books, modern first editions, illustrated volumes and/or modern press publications. Call or write to receive their quarterly newsletter or a specific catalog.

APPENDIX TWO • *Book Fairs*

In order of appearance during the year, here is a listing of the major Manhattan book fairs, selling primarily rare and antiquarian volumes (except where noted) and a good number of used books as well. Call for exact dates.

Greenwich Village Antiquarian Book Fair

P.S. 3, 490 Hudson St (Eighth)
673-3313

last weekend in February

Congregation Rodeph Sholom West Side Antiquarian Book Fair

7 W 83 St (Central Park W)
362-8800

mid-March

New York Antiquarian Book Fair
7th Regiment Armory, Park Ave @ 67 St
777-5218

early May

New York Is Book Country
Fifth Ave between W 48 & 57 Sts
593-3983

mid-September (publishers' booths line Fifth, and you'll find many antiquarian and used book dealers on the side streets)

Metropolitan Arts Antiquarian Book Fair
110 W 19 St (Sixth)
463-0200

early October (Metropolitan has a number of fairs; call for dates)

Hudson Guild Book Sale
441 W 26 St (Ninth)
760-9812

mid-October

Trinity Antiquarian Book Fair
101 W 91 St (Columbus)
873-1650

late October

New York Book Fair to Help the Homeless
Goddard Riverside Community Center
593 Columbus Ave (88)
873-6600

mid-November

Small Press Center Book Fair
20 W 44 St (Sixth)
764-7021

early December (over two hundred small presses display and sell new publications)

And:

Judson Memorial Church Book Fair
55 Washington Sq So (Sullivan)
477-0351

in spring (April or May) and fall (October or November)

APPENDIX THREE · *Libraries*

Mercantile Library
17 E 47 St 10017 (Fifth)
755-6710
M-Sat 10–6

The Mercantile Library was established in 1820 before the advent of the public library. It is still "member's only"; dues are seventy-five dollars per year (seniors and full-time students pay sixty). If you don't want to join, you can still reap some of their literary benefits. A number of books are always for sale on tables and shelves just inside the entrance (outside if the weather's good).

The New York Public Library

In 1895 the Astor Library merged with James Lenox's collection of history, literature, and theology, and with Samuel Tilden's two million dollars, to form the beginning of the New York Public Library. (John Jacob Astor had the first general reference library in the New World, which he dedicated to the working man. Curmudgeon that he was, he kept it open only by day, when the working man was working.) Before entering the main branch of the library (located on the west side of Fifth Ave, between 40th and 42d Street) check out Edward Clark Potter's two marble lions, Fortitude and Patience, and Frederick MacMonnies's fountains, Truth and Beauty. If these aren't impressive enough, inside you'll find more than six million books and seventeen million documents (be aware that this is a research library; none of the material may be removed).

However, each of the eighty branches established by Andrew Carnegie's donation of fifty-two million dollars in 1901 are lending libraries. In addition, many of them even sell books. Here is a listing of those branches that have book sales at designated times (call for exact dates):

Central Children's
  20 W 53 St 10019 (Fifth)
  621-0636

September

Columbus
  742 Tenth Ave 10019 (50)
  586-5098

winter (usually late November or December)

Donnell
  20 W 53 St 10019 (Fifth)
  621-0619

September and first weekend in December

Epiphany
228 E 23 St 10010 (Second)
679-2645

late fall

Mid Manhattan
455 Fifth Ave 10016 (40)
340-0884

every Wednesday

Muhlenberg
209 W 23 St 10011 (Seventh)
924-1585

May

New Amsterdam
9 Murray St 10007 (Broadway)
732-8186

every three months

Riverside
127 Amsterdam Ave 10023 (65)
870-1810

one Monday per month

St. Agnes
444 Amsterdam Ave 10024 (81)
877-4380

May and November

Seward Park
192 E Broadway 10002 (Jefferson)
477-6770

once a month

Sixty-Seventh Street
328 E 67 St 10021 (First)
734-1717

April

The following branches have books for sale which are available for purchase at any time while the library is open. Keep in mind that the pickings may be slim. Call for hours.

Cardinal Cooke
560 Lexington Ave @ 50 St 10022
752-3824

Columbia
521 W 114 St 10027 (Broadway)
864-2530

Countee Cullen
104 W 136 St 10030 (Lenox)
491-2070

Donnell
20 W 53 St 10019 (Fifth)
621-0619

Early Child
66 Leroy St 10014 (Seventh)
929-0815

Epiphany
228 E 23 St 10010 (Second)
679-2645

Fifty-Eighth Street
127 E 58 St 10022 (Park)
759-7358

Fort Washington
535 W 179 St 10033 (St. Nicholas)
927-3533

Hamilton Fish
415 E Houston St 10002 (Avenue D)
673-2290

Hudson Park
66 Leroy St 10014 (Seventh)
243-6876

Jefferson Market
425 Sixth Ave 10014 (10)
243-4334

Kips Bay
446 Third Ave 10016 (31)
683-2520

Macomb's Bridge
2650 Seventh Ave 10039 (152)
281-4900

Ninty-Sixth Street

112 E 96 St 10128 (Park)
289-0908

One Hundred and Twenty-Fifth Street

224 E 125 St 10035 (Second)
534-5050

St. Agnes

444 Amsterdam Ave 10024 (81)
877-4380

Sixty-Seventh Street

328 E 67 St 10021 (First)
734-1717

Tompkins Square

331 E 10 St 10009 (Avenue A)
228-4747

Washington Heights

1000 St. Nicholas Ave 10032 (160)
923-6054

APPENDIX FOUR • *Bookbinders and Restorers*

Check the ANTIQUARIAN listings—many of these dealers also specialize in restoration and binding. Of particular note are APPELFELD GALLERY (p. 61) and WEITZ, WEITZ AND COLEMAN (p. 65).

The following book conservators are open by appointment only; please call during weekday business hours.

Jerilyn Glenn Davis
889-2239

Mindell Dubansky
348-1674

Judith Ivry
677-1015

Jennifer Jestin
799-9222

Jeff Peachey
387-7860

Look under Bookbinders in the yellow pages for a complete listing of businesses specializing in book repair.

Index—By Neighborhood

Index—General

Credits

Photography

Susan Paula Barile: page 16

Lisa Force: pages 2, 7, 10, 12, 18, 28, 30, 35, 57, 186, 191

Mark Saunders: pages 24, 27, 33, 48

Teresa Bonner: pages 20, 36, 38, 42, 44, 45, 81, 92, 138, 140

Illustrations

Illustrations copyright © 1994 Steven Guarnaccia

Logotypes and trademarks courtesy of the bookstores

Designer: Teresa Bonner

Text: Caslon Old Face

Compositor: Maple-Vail

Printer: Maple-Vail

Binder: Maple-Vail